3/23
STRAND PRICE
$5.00

# MY GRANDMOTHER'S GLASS EYE

# MY GRANDMOTHER'S GLASS EYE

A Look at Poetry

Craig Raine

Atlantic Books
London

First published in hardback in Great Britain in 2016 by Atlantic Books,
an imprint of Atlantic Books Ltd.

Copyright © Craig Raine, 2016

The moral right of Craig Raine to be identified as the author
of this work has been asserted by him in accordance with the
Copyright, Designs and Patents Act of 1988.

All rights reserved. No part of this publication may be reproduced,
stored in a retrieval system, or transmitted in any form or by any means,
electronic, mechanical, photocopying, recording, or otherwise,
without the prior permission of both the copyright owner
and the above publisher of this book.

Every effort has been made to trace or contact all copyright-holders.
The author will be pleased to make good any omissions or rectify
any mistakes brought to their attention at the earliest opportunity.

2 4 6 8 10 9 7 5 3 1

A CIP catalogue record for this book is available
from the British Library.

Hardback ISBN 978 1 84887 2899
E-book ISBN 978 1 78239 7434

Printed in Great Britain

Atlantic Books
An imprint of Atlantic Books Ltd
Ormond House
26–27 Boswell Street
London WCIN 3JZ
www.atlantic-books.co.uk

*For Milan and Vera Kundera*

There was no one with more common sense, no stonecutter more obstinate, no manager more lucid or dangerous, than a poet.

GABRIEL GARCÍA MÁRQUEZ: *Love in the Time of Cholera*

# Contents

# Foreword

At the Aldeburgh Poetry Festival in November 2013, I heard Ian McMillan deliver a very funny lecture on surrealist poetry and its unforeseen exotic charge of excitement to a young adolescent boy in Barnsley. McMillan remembered the buzz of a poem about an aeroplane that had propellers like bacon rashers and wings like reinforced lard. I come at the subject of poetry from the opposite direction. The poetry I like, that I prefer, makes sense – either immediately or after extended reflection.

Of course, there are no absolute rules. We all know that feminine rhymes are intrinsically comic. Think of T. S. Eliot's 'The Love Song of J. Alfred Prufrock': 'Should I, after tea and cakes and ices, / Have the strength to force the moment to its crisis?' And yet there is Kipling's 'Harp Song of the Dane Women' – a grim poem of forsaking and threat – where the feminine rhymes are in triplicate eight times, all the way through the poem: 'She [the sea] has no strong white arms to fold you, / But the ten-times-fingering weed to hold you— / Out on the rocks where the tide has rolled you.' Nothing could be more serious. So I know there are no absolute rules in poetry. Genius makes its own rules. But I would say that you have to know the (always provisional) rules in order to break them. I don't believe in accidental innovation. Poetry is, for me, a conscious art. It isn't spontaneous. It is artificial – sometimes in the ways it pretends to be natural and spontaneous. It doesn't just happen.

When Bobby Kennedy came to the Oxford Union, a friend of mine stood next to him in the urinals and noticed he was wearing TV make-up. As far as Kennedy was concerned, he was on TV all the time and wanted to look as natural as possible. He will serve as a figure for poetry.

In this book, I examine poetry's relationship to music and the different ways in which music 'means' and poetry means. Many of my examples, too, are taken from prose. Unapologetically. In *The Guardian* (25 January 2014) Adam Foulds, who is a poet and a novelist, observed that many people who used 'poetic' as a criticism of the novel – meaning over-written and over-sensitive – displayed 'a not very accurate understanding of what good poetry is'. I agree with his addendum: 'Great poetry such as William Wordsworth's *The Prelude* is not "poetic" in that sense, in that it is full of the brilliant accuracies you find in good prose.' Brilliant accuracies and intensity – qualities shared by the best poetry and prose.

I am against poetry which is vague, pretentious and exaggerated. I am against neither difficult poetry nor pellucid poetry. But poetry has to be cogent in the end. Surrealism, for example, is a cogent strategy of incoherence. If you say propellers are like rashers of bacon, you know you are flouting sense. It isn't a complicated strategy, and it's one with diminishing returns. However differently the finger is placed, the same button is pressed and no one answers the door.

And poetry is naturally various. Each poem should have a unique form – whether it is written as a sonnet, quatrains, sestina, or any other given form. There is inevitably a secret formal agenda, a shared harmony, concord. Here are five fairly radical examples of what I mean. Christopher Reid's poem 'A Whole School of Bourgeois Primitives', a description of a house and garden, is written in stripes – the deckchairs, interference on the television, the cat's pyjamas, jockeys' silks. My poem 'A Martian Sends a Postcard Home' has the form of a postcard: its observations are laconic and discrete; weather is a standard feature, a required field. 'Mist is when the sky is tired of flight', 'Rain is when the earth is television', are versions of the postcard's statutory meteorology. James Fenton's 'Lines for Translation into Any Language' is about the everyday surrealism of war in Vietnam and it has the numbered form of an examination paper: '1. I saw that the shanty town had grown over the graves and that the crowd lived among the memorials.' Diogenes lived, naked, in a barrel. Paul Muldoon's '[Diogenes]' in *Madoc* is a trio of pseudo-barrels, a poem of Diogenes decorum: Sara puts her hand into a meal-ark; Southey lies in a claw-foot bath; and a snail mimics Diogenes in a barrel. 'A tongue-in-cheek snail goes meticulously / across a mattock's // blade-end.' Less radically, Carol Ann Duffy's 'Stuffed', a poem about a child molester and soft-toy maker, rhymes the same sound twelve times – an aural index of the obsessive speaker. You can read the full text of these five poems, and others, in the appendix to this book.

My first chapters consider the word 'poetry' when it is used unselfconsciously, without our thinking what it is. I want to examine our unexamined assumptions about poetry – and correct them. Why do we wear ties? The answer may surprise you. To hide the buttons down our shirt fronts. As if the buttons themselves were naughty, halfway to nakedness, immodest. The aim of this book is modest. I want to show you poetry's buttons. I want to bare its devices.

# Preface

## Four Demonstrations

Must all be vail'd, while he that reads, divines,
Catching the sense at two removes?
George Herbert: 'Jordan'

I want to begin with two poems I like – one easy to understand, the other notoriously difficult. The easy one first: Ted Hughes's 'New Year exhilaration'.

> On the third day
> Finds its proper weather. Pressure
> Climbing and the hard blue sky
> Scoured by gales. The world's being
> Swept clean. Twigs that can't cling
> Go flying, last leaves ripped off
> Bowl along roads like daring mice. Imagine
> The new moon hightide sea under this
> Rolling of air-weights. Exhilaration
> Lashes everything. Windows flash,
> White houses dazzle, fields glow red.
> Seas pour in over the land, invisible maelstroms
> Set the house-joints creaking. Every twig-end
> Writes its circles and the earth
> Is massaged with roots. The power of hills

Hold their bright faces in the wind-shine.
The hills are being honed. The river
Thunders like a factory, its weirs
Are tremendous engines. People
Walk precariously, the whole landscape
Is imperilled, like a tarpaulin
With the wind under it. 'It nearly
Blew me up the chymbley!' And a laugh
Blows away like a hat.

We have no difficulty reading this poem. The wind has the force
of an invisible sea. We can feel the surge of invention about
halfway through. Sure, 'Every twig-end / Writes its circles'
captures the commotion observantly. But the genius is there
in those roots *massaging* the earth, *working the earth*, the counter-intuitive comparison of the river to a factory, the roar of the
weirs. And then the idea that the landscape itself might blow
away, a comic, hyperbolic apocalypse, followed by the comic
throw-away end – the laugh and the hat. That surge is the exhilaration of the title.

Sylvia Plath's 'Ariel' is, by contrast, a difficult poem. The
note by Ted Hughes, in Plath's *Collected Poems*, informs us Ariel
was a horse she rode in Devon. It seems a simple enough fact.
But the name 'Ariel' is dense with connotation, explosive with
implication. The literal is quickly eroded. Most readers will
think first of the spirit in Shakespeare's *The Tempest*, a creature
the opposite of the grossly corporeal Caliban. This fits a gallop
in which the rider sheds her body: 'White / Godiva, I unpeel...'
But there is more. The title, 'Ariel', the *OED* tells us, is the name
given to Jerusalem in the Old Testament. It means the lion of
god. The Larousse Encyclopedia supplies another sacred lion.
In Babylonian-Assyrian mythology, Ishtar is the goddess of

morning and evening, of love and war. As goddess of battles she is frequently depicted riding her sacred animal, the lion.

On the face of it, this allusion seems unlikely. Shakespeare's *The Tempest* is one thing, Babylonian-Assyrian mythology quite another – the relatively near-at-hand versus the far-fetched. We see the stooped academic stopped over a dusty tome dredged from the depths of the library stacks.

How do we know that Plath had Ishtar in mind?

First, because she and her husband, Ted Hughes, were adepts in mythology. It was a passion for them. They were immersed in the scattered arcana of myth, gripped by the quest for a universal symbolism. To them, every shard seemed to promise completion, a sacred wholeness. Hughes's book-length study of Shakespeare – *Shakespeare and the Goddess of Complete Being* – attempts to identify the mythic template underlying all of Shakespeare's work.

Secondly, because Plath mentions Ishtar in 'Last Words', an earlier poem written in 1961, whose last line is: 'And the shine of these small things sweeter than the face of Ishtar.' Neither Plath nor Hughes would think Ishtar too recondite. Myths were their stock in trade. 'Ariel' begins in darkness and stasis. Then it accelerates into the red eye of the sun, 'the cauldron of morning'.

It is a poem about suicide.

> And I
> Am the arrow,
>
> The dew that flies
> Suicidal...

But it is a poem in which suicide is sacrifice, self-sacrifice, for a purpose. When Ishtar goes to the underworld to rescue

Tammuz, god of the harvest, she has to pass through seven gates, at each stripping off jewellery and clothing until she is naked:

> White
> Godiva, I unpeel—
> Dead hands, dead stringencies.

You see the Hughes–Plath mind-set at work – the way Ishtar morphs into Lady Godiva, an illustration of the essential unity and interchangeability of myth. For both poets, myths were versions of a fundamental psychic DNA, a great universal formula.

Sylvia Plath's *oeuvre* is predicated on the idea of death and rebirth. *The Bell Jar* is a series of pseudo-deaths and rebirths. For example, Esther has a skiing accident which almost kills her but returns her to the status of a baby: she hurtles towards 'the pebble at the bottom of the well, the white sweet baby cradled in its mother's belly'.

In 'Ariel', the death imagery is there in the 'Black sweet blood mouthfuls' – at once blackberries and a quasi-hemlock. And also in the 'Dead hands, dead stringencies'. These are supplanted by the harvest growth, foaming to wheat, and the baby's birth-cry.

Ariel, the *OED* additionally tells us, means 'altar', 'the fire-hearth of God'. Where Ishtar might sacrifice herself to save Tammuz. Or, in this update, this adaptation, Sylvia Plath might sacrifice herself to save Ted.

We need to know that Sylvia Plath tried to kill herself several times in her life and that, although she asked her husband to leave, she was inconsolable – 'Once one has seen God, what is the remedy?' This line from 'Mystic' epitomises her uncompromising, extreme romantic temperament. Without these facts, the poems are impossible to interpret. While she was alive, and for a time after her death, they couldn't be revealed. 'Sheep in Fog', for example, is a figure for self-obliteration. Sheep in fog are invisible. But you can't read a poem like this on Radio 3 and introduce it by saying you are drawn to suicide. Instead, Plath said: 'In this poem, the speaker's horse is proceeding at a slow, cold walk down a hill of macadam to the stable at the bottom. It is December. It is foggy. In the fog there are sheep.' True – as far as it goes. Which isn't far enough.

From these two very different poems, one by Ted Hughes, one by Sylvia Plath; one accessible, one encrypted, I draw this conclusion. To understand, to read poems, you use undogmatically whatever is necessary, whatever your intelligence suggests. The only fatal thing is to believe poems are without meaning – sense in the ordinary sense.

According to Hugh Haughton in *The Poetry of Derek Mahon*, 'A Disused Shed in Co. Wexford' is 'one of the most complex political poems of the twentieth century'.

It isn't a political poem at all.

Haughton, like Tom Paulin in *The Secret Life of Poems*, has succumbed to the prejudice that all Northern Irish poems must be about the Troubles. For Paulin, 'A Disused Shed in Co. Wexford' is a 'very subtle and finely tuned response' to the Troubles, in which Mahon 'manages to avoid the self-conscious persona of poet commenting on the Troubles'. In other words, the poem's secret is that it is really about the Troubles, though it seems not to be.

Actually, Paulin has very little to say about the meaning of the poem. He mentions 'the Holocaust theme'. He mentions 'the theme of aesthetic anxiety'. He doesn't mention the binding theme – those mushrooms which have been abandoned by their creator. Mahon has written a poem about a world in which there is no God. 'Let the god not abandon us / Who have come so far in darkness and in pain.'

John Banville is nearer the heart of the poem – roughly at its sternum – when he says it is 'a great elegy for the lost ones of the world'. The mushrooms are the doomed of Pompeii and Treblinka, the victims of the *Ancien Régime* in pre-revolutionary France – all analogues that are explicitly evoked. It is an elegy for the lost and the suffering. It is also something more.

What does the first line mean? 'Even now there are places where a thought might grow – ' It means places where the spiritual, where the idea, might make itself materially manifest, might become incarnate. It raises the idea of creation, of animated matter – comparable to man, the *thinking* animal. Mahon's mushrooms, therefore, are the embodiment of a *second* creation of thinking matter, after humans – a poetic fiction, thinking mushrooms.

'Even now there are places where a thought might grow...' *Even now*. It is difficult to hear this without summoning the Third Priest in T. S. Eliot's *Murder in the Cathedral*:

> The critical moment
> That is always now, and here.
> Even now, in sordid particulars
> The eternal design may appear.

I think that Mahon had Eliot's lines in mind – consciously or unconsciously, it doesn't matter – when he considered the idea of the eternal design *disappearing*. The mushrooms 'lift frail heads in gravity and *good faith*' [my italics].

'A Disused Shed in Co. Wexford' is a very good poem and a very clear poem if it is read correctly. But some contemporary readers prefer confusion. In *The Guardian* (15 March 2014), Fiona Sampson was reviewing Lavinia Greenlaw's version of Chaucer's *Troilus and Criseyde*: Sampson ended by invoking 'the mystery that is the mark of real poetry'.

Primo Levi's essay against this trend, 'On Obscure Writing', has its moments of argumentative hysteria: 'it is not by chance that the two least decipherable German poets, Trakl and Celan, both died as suicides.' However, Levi is right, I believe, to insist that obscurity, even if it isn't a short-cut to suicide, isn't in itself a virtue. Waller's 'Goe Lovely Rose' is a great, unforgettable lyric and not in the least obscure. It works in the tradition of the *carpe diem*, paying its elegant and expected compliments, urging the beloved to relent, until it suddenly shocks us with the curt command, 'Then die'. Die as a demonstration of mortality, of how quickly the quick become the dead. Anyone who can read feels the force of this injunction. I think T. S. Eliot has something to answer for when he prescribed, as a condition for poetry in his time, that it should be 'difficult'. But he has been punished by several generations of academic readers happy to import confusion, complication and incoherence into his poetry.

Edward Thomas's 'Old Man', as its title might lead you to expect, looks, in its last line, directly at death: 'Only an avenue, dark, nameless, without end.' The whole poem is about the two names of the same herb – Lad's-love and Old Man – and the way in which we lose the specifics of the first in the impaired recall of the other. Early love, lad's love, is lost love, irrecoverable in its essentials: 'As for myself, / Where first I met the bitter scent is lost.' Edward Thomas gifts us a Proustian moment, a madeleine moment, whose source remains stubbornly out of sight. The old man of the poem tries 'Once more to think what it is I am remembering, / Always in vain.' The qualia, the sensation, the detail, the actuality of love have gone missing, 'Yet I would rather give up others more sweet, / With no meaning, than this bitter one.' It might be Tennyson feeling the bruised aura left by Rosa Baring, the girl who deserted him to marry Robert Duncombe Shafto.

The herb has two names, twice repeated, at the beginning of the poem and almost at the very end, but the title, 'Old Man', decides the controlling epithet. I invoke Tennyson deliberately because 'Old Man' is Edward Thomas's palimpsest, his cover version of Tennyson's 'Tears, Idle Tears'. 'I know not what they [the idle tears] mean', writes Tennyson. Nevertheless, they are 'deep as love, / Deep as first love, and wild with all regret.'

For Glyn Maxwell, in *On Poetry*, the Thomas poem is about a child growing away from its parent – an interpretation he enforces with rhetoric: 'And now, with what barely breathed and creeping terror does he place himself there, where she [the daughter] was just now, where he was long ago, where they both were long ago. Nowhere in all of poetry do I find an agonising abyssal emptiness such as Thomas has in the two words "Once more" – he tries to make the rest of that line last forever.' The line in question is: 'Once more to think what it is I am remembering'. It won't bear the amplified baloney Maxwell is determined to balance on it.

Bad readers, like the poor, are always with us. And their badness takes the form of the complacent confusion they bring to poetry. Poetry isn't diminished by clarity.

# Introduction

## *Poetry as an Art*

You remember that moment in Anthony Minghella's film *The English Patient* when a penitent Ralph Fiennes is sewing a tear he has passionately made in Kristin Scott Thomas's adulterous underwear? A great ironic moment, exploiting and acknowledging the cliché of the bodice-ripper. When I was Poetry Editor at Faber, a sales rep called Gill Hess asked why the firm couldn't publish a bodice-ripper. I answered him: 'Because no one at Fabers knows the difference between a good bodice-ripper and a bad bodice-ripper.' There is a difference. Another publisher recently explained to me the difference between a literary novel and a novel that might be sold in Tesco. It was not that the popular novel was *badly* written and the literary novel *well* written. It was that there was *no writing at all* in the popular novel. A popular novel should not distract the reader with writing. Reading a popular novel should be like watching television. Whereas poetry is *all writing*. It is the opposite of watching television. Attention must be paid, as Linda Loman says of her husband Willy Loman in *Death of a Salesman*.

On the other hand, poetry has to sell itself – *without selling out*.

How does it sell itself? In 'Writing Poetry is an Unnatural Act...', some notes for an essay on poetry, Elizabeth Bishop meditates on the self-evident artificiality of poetry – and the need to persuade the reader that it is spontaneous. You might think there is a spectrum of spontaneity – with the bunk-side manner of Frost at one extreme and the Tennyson of 'The Lady of Shalott' or Dylan Thomas's candidly artificial 'Altarwise by Owl-Light' at the other. This is true, but *all* poetry is artificial. Elizabeth Bishop's image for this hybridity, for this negotiation between the artificial and the apparently spontaneous, is her grandmother's glass eye and her grandmother's other, seeing eye, the former often arbitrarily, implausibly angled. In 'The Three Voices of Poetry', T. S. Eliot said dramatic poetry should be as natural as possible, the way people *would* speak *if* people spoke in verse. There is a space between reality and its representation that has to be negotiated and minimised. This space requires what Coleridge called 'the willing suspension of disbelief'. Contrivance requires connivance: it helps if, as a reader, you have an educated squint. Occasionally, you encounter undergraduates who are theoretically outraged that Wordsworth thought of his *Lyrical Ballads* as 'the real language of men' – an absurdity, they argue, because real men don't speak in verse. As if Wordsworth were unaware of this fact.

Not simply connivance, also pleasure in that contrivance. It seems odd to me that we are still trapped in the idea that art and sincerity are logically incompatible. It begins with Dr Johnson on Milton's elegy 'Lycidas' and the pastoral: 'where there is leisure for fiction, there is little grief.' We can test this, using Thomas Wyatt's poem 'In Mourning Wise Since Daily I Increase', his great elegy for Brereton, Smeaton, Norris, Weston and George Boleyn, all those executed for their alleged adultery with Anne Boleyn. Wyatt was also arrested. He was known to have had a romantic attachment to Anne before she married Henry VIII. But he was released without charge. There is a moment of great art, of frank art, in the poem: 'the axe is home, your heads be in the street'. The witty play here is on 'home' and eviction, 'in the street' – where the heads of the executed were displayed on spikes. Wyatt says the paper he writes on is wet with tears. But we do not need this asseveration to believe in Wyatt's sincerity. The writing of the poem itself tells us he was sincere. It was a potentially fatal act to sympathise with the executed. Wyatt was risking his life, as he must have known, having been in the Tower so recently himself. And yet he writes, with supreme art, 'the axe is home, your heads be in the street'.

I want to argue that poetry needs no excuse, no special pleading, no vanishing cream to be applied to its art. It is like theatre, where we relish the artificiality, the equivalences. By equivalences I mean the way theatre bares the device, is candidly artful, when it transfers to the stage something impossible – the blinding of Gloucester, the suicide of Madame Butterfly. Or someone walking through a waterfall. In 1989, Peter Sellars directed a production of Velimir Khlebnikov's play *Zangezi – A Supersaga in 20 Planes* at the Boston Museum of Fine Arts. He was using Paul Schmidt's translation, which I read beforehand. With this preparation, I was possibly the only member of the audience who realised what was happening when Zangezi walked through the waterfall. To the other members of the audience, the actor simply shook and wafted up a huge sheet of cling film until it was head-height and he could step under it. Sellars hit it with every light in the house as the actor batted the cling film with both hands, as if forcing his way through a torrent. The film of Keita Asari's 1986 Milan production of *Madame Butterfly* is another case in point. As in kabuki, stagehands are dressed in black so that we know they are invisible. Here, Butterfly's seppuku involved a white sheet with four 'invisible' stage-hands at each corner. She knelt in the centre of the sheet and stabbed herself with a closed Japanese fighting fan. Which she then opened, pleat by pleat, in pulses, gasps, rhythmic bumps. Each pleat was blood-red. And as she knelt 'bleeding', the stage-hands eased the four sections of white sheet towards them to disclose a red under-sheet that grew and grew. You could dismiss this as contrivance. It is contrived. But it is also inspired. It is a *great* illusion.

Recently I was on Radio 3's *Essential Classics*. A feature of the show is called 'Personal Shopper'. After choosing your own guest selection of records, the presenter Sarah Walker finds a CD she thinks you might like. For me, she chose a piece by Louis Spohr, a contemporary of Beethoven, in a later nineteenth-century version, arranged for bassoon. When I heard it in the studio, I couldn't hear the player taking breaths. But on headphones later, I could hear the breaths – and the music was transfigured. Breaths are not part of music. You wouldn't hear them in the concert hall. You might see them. When I heard the breaths, the device was bared, the means exposed. Breath, lungs, blood in the face, effort, tensile lips, eyes following the score, ribcage lifting – these are the means and they show us that the sublime disembodied sound we hear is an illusion and a transcendence.

Instead of being embarrassed by poetry's artificiality, we should glory in its illusions, its metaphors, its images, its rhythms, its form, its equivalences.

And we should revel in its care, its often invisible care. When theatre directors work on a play with the actors, they spend six to eight weeks rehearsing. This is partly so that, when it comes to the first night, the actors will have the moves in their muscles and the words lodged in their lips and tongues and palates – an automism that overrides nerves. When Howard Davies directed Christopher Hampton's play *The Talking Cure* at the National

Theatre, James Hazeldine, the actor playing Freud, died. The Scottish actor Bill Paterson was brought in, learned the lines and the moves in a day, went on and performed perfectly. As he came off-stage for the last time on opening night, he resigned and refused to continue the run. He was too terrified. That is what rehearsals are for. They are also a process by which director and actors consider the detail, this detail, that detail, the details, till every detail is right. It matters. This is why the director gives notes – correcting the details, adjusting an emphasis, reminding the actors of what has been agreed in the rehearsal room, about tone, delivery, gesture, speed, energy. Often a director will be dismayed at what has gone wrong, detail that has gone missing – although the audience registers little of this perfectionism. Except subliminally.

The same is true of poetry, which is an art of micro-adjustments – of this word rather than that, this rationed repetition, this euphony, this calculated dissonance, this decision to sacrifice a sound effect to clarity. For instance, in Marvell's 'The Garden', we read about 'luscious clusters' of the vine, which 'crush' themselves against the mouth. The repeated vowel 'u', the short 'u', isn't an accident. It is mimetic. Compare Tennyson's 'Laborious orient ivory, sphere in sphere' in The Princess to invoke those interlocking carved ivory circles. A smaller example, the phrase 'modest breasts': modest meaning 'small', possibly 'concealed'. In this case, the breasts are exposed, so the idea of pudeur is invoked ironically. We are left with 'modest' as 'small'. The proximity of one small breast to another small breast is mirrored in the close internal rhyme, 'modest breasts'. The potential crudity of the mimesis is offset by the inexactitude of the rhyme. I know all this is true because it comes from a poem I wrote yesterday. I am giving you my working, as mathematicians say. The reader may not be aware of all the invisible mending, but he knows when there's a tear or a hole.

For centuries, poets have had an implicit contract with the reader that poems mean something or some things, that they aren't exercises in endless deferral of meaning. One exception is Dylan Thomas whose syntax often deliberately forestalls resolution. (We read him for the other, clear passages: 'And the sabbath rang slowly / In the pebbles of the holy streams.') Mostly the reader is entitled to expect resolution and meaning. Poetry isn't a perverse crossword puzzle, without answers, designed to divert setter and solver until eternity. But we are wary of equating poetry with the shallow, solvable puzzle. We should be equally wary, however, of equating poetry with espionage, requiring an Enigma machine and a team of code-breakers from Bletchley Park. Think about Blake's 'The Clod and the Pebble', a perfectly simple parable of human behaviour – simple, but profound. Profundity doesn't always entail difficulty and an interpretative oubliette. On the other hand, 'the moment in the draughty church at smokefall' in Eliot's 'Burnt Norton' presents a candid difficulty. What is 'smokefall'? Out of the several possible answers – London particulars, dense yellow fogs, dusk – the most satisfying answer is 'incense'. We are often told that there are no right answers where poetry is concerned. But 'smokefall' for 'incense' is a beautiful poetic re-consideration and re-description of incense – at once an exact fit, a perfect fit, and a complete re-invention.

Compare Emily Dickinson's flower in 'I could bring You Jewels': we aren't told the subject is a flower, its identity is never named; it is 'this little Blaze / Flickering to itself – in the Meadow'. You might plausibly think she intends a butterfly. Compare Robert Browning's 'James Lee's Wife' in which the butterflies are blots of flame. What resolves the dilemma in favour of a flower? Firstly, Emily Dickinson's common practice, well-attested, of sending a flower with an accompanying poem. And there is, too, a contrast, a hint of paradox, between the concept of 'blaze', however 'little', and the concept of 'flicker'. The tension between the two is resolved by the new context. Singled out, the flower blazes. In the field, with other nature, it flickered in the breeze. More, it flickered 'to itself', a figure for loneliness, whereas now it has been kindled by the loved person who receives it to a passionate blaze.

Dickinson gives us all the information we need to get to the destination. Auden said that poetry makes nothing happen. Poetry itself doesn't *happen*. However spontaneous it seems, the flower has been arranged.

Is there any middle ground between poetry with answers and poetry without answers? Sometimes the answer is poised perfectly between possibilities – clear but undecided – for example, Ezra Pound's 'In a Station of the Metro', a classic imagist poem.

In Richard Sieburth's edition of Pound's *Selected Poems and Translations*, the spacing of the poem is that of its first magazine publication.

> The apparition  of these faces  in the crowd  :
> Petals  on a wet, black  bough  .

Pound's theories of Chinese poetry, taken from Ernest Fenollosa, were centred on the concrete pictorial nature of the ideogram. Pound described this poem as 'hokku-like'. It shares brevity with the haiku and perhaps this spacing is meant to reproduce (loosely) the three phrases of the haiku of five, seven and five syllables. Perhaps. I think it is an example of concrete poetry. Just as William Carlos Williams's poem about a wheelbarrow mimics the shape of the wheelbarrow in each stanza in a *carmen figuratum*:

a red wheel
barrow

Equally, Pound is representing the faces and the space separating them.

We could say that Pound's title definitively locates the reader in the Paris underground. On the other hand, we could describe Pound's evocation of a modern transport system as transporting us elsewhere. Just as the word 'transport' moves semantically between the idea of moving vehicles and the idea of joy, so this scene at the metro moves between the underground and the underworld. It is an equation made by Saul Bellow in *The Adventures of Augie March*, Chapter XXIII: 'This was just before dawn, by the *descent-into-hell* stairs of the subway…' [my italics]

It seems an obvious poetic move and one that Seamus Heaney makes twice. In 'The Underground', the opening poem of *Station Island*, Heaney remembers running to the Proms in the underground tunnels of Exhibition Road. The buttons on his wife's coat are popping off one by one as they hurry to the concert in the Royal Albert Hall. Heaney remembers not daring to look back – a reference to Orpheus going back, unsuccessfully, to rescue his wife Eurydice from the underworld. In *District and Circle*, the title poem candidly equates the Circle line with the circles of the underworld: the dead, the ghosts, are there in the reflections Heaney sees in the carriage windows.

I think something similar is intended in Pound's poem – a hint, though, a sketch, a ghosting of the modern with the ancient pagan underworld. In 'The Return', Pound imagines the return of the pagan gods – and how enfeebled they are, these survivors of a defeated world. Yeats presents in 'The Wanderings of Oisin' a similar vision of paganism's defeat by Christianity.

The key word is 'apparition' – a sudden manifestation *and* a synonym for 'ghost'. Then there is the 'wet, black bough', ghosted by the golden bough torn by Aeneas to gain passage into the underworld in Book 6 of the *Aeneid*. Not the golden bough proper, but an echo, a diminuendo, an entropic version, fading even as we find it. The bough isn't an exact, certain parallel, but the disturbing, tentative hint of one.

So, poetry can be difficult, yet equally it can be simple, but, unless it is automatic writing, it is always shaped by authorial intention.

Poetry is an art. It is artifice. A sonnet isn't a sunset. That's why poets were once known as makers. What kind of an art is it?

A sexual analogy, suggested by something Seamus Heaney said to me about *Finnegans Wake* when I interviewed him in 1981 for a BBC programme about Joyce. He said Joyce's words were 'slippy with delight'. There is an element of heightened, erotic excitement to poetry. Poetry excites the prosaic, whetting the words, working the words to a climax.

# Chapter One

---

# *Vagueness and Accuracy*

In *Joseph Anton: A Memoir*, Salman Rushdie wonders what he, an atheist, means when he uses the word 'soul'. Is 'soul' a kind of poetry?

I am against poetry. Or rather I am against poetry in the sense that Salman Rushdie uses it in *Joseph*. By poetry we – we the masses – mean something vague, something untrue, something uplifting, something beautiful, something so eloquent it isn't for everyday. The word 'poetry' is up there with 'soul'. And I am against it. The painter Claude Lorrain – Claude, as he is usually known – is automatically praised for the poetry of his painting. By this, critics mean stage curtains of umber foliage disclosing a pretty scene of ruins populated by a few anonymous archaic classical figures in pastoral drapes, sometimes semi-nude. In 2011–2012, the Ashmolean Museum in Oxford mounted a Claude exhibition. It was called 'The Enchanted Landscape', a title that tells you everything about the consensus of art historians. On loan from the ninth Duke of Buccleuch, however, came a big oil, *Coast View*, 1663. It had all the balance you expect from a Claude – two matching classical buildings at each side of the picture, the left in shade, the right in sunlight. Between them is a boat-maker's yard, with an anchor, canvas and cordage, but mainly full of planks. On the far right of the picture, there is a man with a blue jacket, red knee breeches, a straw hat and a

cloak over his left shoulder. His back is to the viewer. He is looking down. His legs are apart. Look for his hands and they are
invisible. He is taking a piss. There is no mention of this in the
catalogue. *That* is the kind of poetry I like – uncensored poetry,
not the poetry which is an edited version of reality, poetry which
occludes the prosaic; something bogus, something mendacious.
In *Seeing Things*, Seamus Heaney examines these imaginative,
temporary, tempting truths. His title is ironic – suggesting illusion, scepticism, and its opposite, the visionary. In other words,
Heaney is interested in the ambiguous area implied by another
title, *True at First Light*, Hemingway's posthumous work, whose
title is probably the best thing in it.

Poetry is routinely said to be the highest of the arts. Unless,
of course, we are being told by Walter Pater and Oscar Wilde
that all art aspires to the condition of music. This chapter
addresses both poetry and music – and the role of meaning
in both. How does music mean? How does poetry mean? I
wonder whether music and poetry are situated at the apex of
the arts as a result of the way meaning is thought to work in
both arts. They are thought to be great because both music
and poetry appear at once unspecific and all-encompassing. If
a single meaning cannot be assigned with any conviction, then
perhaps this is because both arts are too profound to be para-
phrased. T. S. Eliot says, in 'Poetry and Drama', that 'there is a
fringe of indefinite extent, of feeling which we can only detect,
so to speak, out of the corner of the eye'. He adds, conflat-
ing the music of poetry and music itself: 'this peculiar range of
sensibility can be expressed by dramatic poetry, at its moments
of greatest intensity. At such moments, we touch the border of
those feelings which only music can express.'

Music and poetry have completely different ways of meaning. I want to separate these Siamese twins.

Let me explain my 'methodology'. Rather like a linguistic philosopher, I want to examine the semantic field around the word 'poetry', when it appears unselfconsciously, used confidently and unproblematically by writers who assume they know what the word means. I want to begin with sightings of poetry well away from Parnassus, sudden appearances, incognito, enigmatic, radiant in Ray-Bans, in the pages of the novel. What do these tell us about the Muse, about poetry?

Prose practitioners tend to have elevated assumptions about poetry. E. M. Forster in *Howards End* reaches reflexively for 'poetry' when he wants to invoke afflatus. Helen Schlegel and Paul Wilcox kiss at the beginning of the novel. Nothing comes of it, in fact, but Forster, poor starved Forster, hungrily promotes this fleeting contact: the 'poetry of that kiss' transports the participants and the 'doors of heaven were opened'. (I think Forster has Psalm XXIV in mind: 'Lift up your heads, O ye gates, and be ye lift up, ye everlasting doors; and the King of glory shall come in.' J. D. Salinger's instinct is identical when he has Boo Boo Glass invoke 'Raise high the roof beam, carpenters' for the wedding of Seymour Glass and Muriel Fedder. The Authorised Version means the uplift is official.) Poetry, its afflatus, leaves the novelist a little bit breathless. And breathlessness is next to godliness. Evidently.

Jean-Dominique Bauby's *The Diving-Bell and the Butterfly* is a painstaking account of locked-in syndrome – written, letter by letter, by blinking an eyelid, the only part of his paralysed body Bauby was able to move. A nurse recited the alphabet and Bauby blinked to stop her at the intended letter. He was hospitalised at Berck-sur-Mer. On two occasions he was driven to Paris.

On his first visit, he is moved by the piercing immediacy of Paris: 'I shed a few tears as we passed the corner café where I used to drop in for a bite. I can weep discreetly. People think my eye is watering.' The second time he visits Paris, however, he is unmoved. Reality has been displaced by a simulacrum, something beautiful but unreal:

> The second time I went to Paris, four months later, I was unmoved by it. The streets were decked out in summer finery, but for me it was still winter, and what I saw through the ambulance windows was just a movie background. Filmmakers call the process a rear screen projection, with the hero's car speeding along a road which unrolls behind him on a studio wall. Hitchcock films owe much of their poetry to the use of this process in its early, unperfected stages.

The poetry of back projection. What exactly does that amount to? How does the flagrant unreality relate to poetry? When we talk about a poetic fiction, we mean a fiction which is transparent, an illusion tolerated and benign. For example, in *Granta* 112, there was a story by Nadeem Aslam called 'Leila in the Wilderness' which included this sentence: 'the next song he'd make up for her would be about a lamp in a room where two lovers met – so engrossed did the flame become in watching them that it continued to burn when the oil finished'. Wallace Stevens is a great theorist of poetic fiction, what he calls 'the supreme fiction': 'the final belief is to believe in a fiction, which you know to be a fiction, there being nothing else. The exquisite truth is to know that it is a fiction and that you believe in it willingly.' Likewise, poetic justice is an ideal state where the punishment perfectly fits the crime. There is something ideal in the air to which we safely succumb because we also acknowledge its unreality: it is, most of all, *vague*. The 'poetic' is something deprived of quiddity, deprived of reality. For Jean-Dominique, poetry is fugitive, fake, frail, freighted with the *aura of meaning*. Lewis Carroll's 'Jabberwocky' flaunts this faint semantic perfume. After listening, Alice is nonplussed: '"It seems very pretty," she said when she had finished it, "but it's *rather* hard to understand!" (You see she didn't like to confess, even to herself, that she couldn't make it out at all.) "Somehow it seems to fill my head with ideas – only I don't know exactly what they are!"' The comedian Stanley Unwin was another exacting purveyor of inexactitude, giving us 'Unwinese', a fluent pseudo-language – the sound of sense without the sense itself. Unwin, who died in 2002, was often billed as Professor Stanley Unwin, which tells us something about the idea of the professor in the popular mind – a person so intellectually elevated as to be unintelligible.

The *aura of meaning*. That is what constitutes poetry for many amateurs. Human beings like the drama of incompletion, of incomprehensibility, of unintelligibility. We have a deep tolerance for being baffled, a patience tinged with pleasure: we watch a Jason Bourne film *because* its narrative is fundamentally occluded, drugged en route as we are by episodes of inexplicable excitement. Coleridge, the inventor of the fragment as a poetic form, said of Edmund Kean's acting: it was 'like reading Shakespeare by flashes of lightning'. (Now you see it, now you don't.) Coleridge's compliment to Kean's bravura was brilliantly, unjustly, recycled by Oscar Wilde as a put-down for Kipling: reading Kipling, said Wilde, was like being 'seated under a palm reading life by superb flashes of vulgarity'. 'Kubla Khan', Coleridge's most famous fragment, has held us with its aura of meaning for two centuries. But only because we are convinced it means something – whereas it is in fact a fake antique, a copy of the fragments found in Bishop Percy's *Reliques of Ancient English Poetry*. It is costume jewellery, brilliant, dazzling, but actually paste. (I know: heresy.)

Ezra Pound's 'Papyrus' is even more candidly fragmented:

Spring......
Too long......
Gongula......

We don't need to know that Gongula was a disciple of Sappho. We need only appreciate the name was once specific and is now three syllables set against silence. Pound's poem is precise in its occlusions, clear in its suggestiveness, up front about its unique form – it is written in remnants.

The intermittent, the aura of meaning, spiced with the explicit, is to be found in many Bob Dylan songs. Dylan changed his surname from Zimmerman to Dylan in homage to Dylan Thomas, with whom he has much in common. Thomas's poetry has a weakness for rhetoric, for the grand gesture, for drinks on the house, for intoxication, for the visionary. Sometimes Thomas is successful, as he is in 'Fern Hill'. There, sleep and night end and the farm is depicted as a returning wanderer, white with dew instead of dust. A brilliant touch – this wanderer is gifted a cock on his shoulder. The imaginative act of anthropomorphism, the bold metaphorical transformation, is perfect and confident. It might be Dickens, or Disney, or Emily Dickinson. Think of Dickinson's 'I'll tell you how the Sun rose', in which the sunset becomes the 'little yellow boys and girls' going to school with a 'dominie in gray'. There is a comic spirit at work, a cartoon spirit, brilliantly simplifying. When Thomas is in this vein, he is incomparable: a steeple seen in the distance becomes a wet, shining snail. But at the other pole are obfuscated, rhyme-led sequences, all sound and no sense, like

'Altarwise by Owl-Light', written for the code-breakers at Chel-
tenham GCHQ. I think that Thomas wrote like this because he
internalised T. S. Eliot's *ex cathedra* statement (in 'The Metaphysical Poets') that poetry must be prepared 'to dislocate if
necessary language into meaning'. A dangerous directive for
Dylan Thomas – and a disastrous example for Bob Dylan, who
seems to have followed Thomas following Eliot.

Some Dylan songs are feeble. One example, from 'When
the Ship Comes In', singled out by the brilliant Louis Menand
in the *New Yorker* (4 September 2006). It uses the otiose 'for to'
construction better than 'to' or 'in order to'. As it were: I took
my pen for to write a book.

Some Dylan songs are intelligible and tough, like 'It Ain't
Me, Babe'. Which is a great song, not a poem, and a paean to
male romantic reluctance, the refusal to be coerced by romantic
blackmail, the male keeping his options open.

With his nasal *Sprechgesang* and his addiction to rhyme,
Dylan is the father of rap. But he is himself the offspring of
Thomas. There is a character in Brian Friel's play *Translations*
who says '"uncertainty in meaning is incipient poetry"'. Who
said that?' It could have been Dylan Thomas. It could have been
Bob Dylan. It is the misguided guiding principle of both. A
Dylan song like 'I Want You' has a simple chorus. It has all the
difficulty of the Beatles' 'I Wanna Hold Your Hand'. The chorus
is the spar we cling to in a welter of nonsense, of 'poetry', for
stanza after stanza.

You could say 'I Want You' means, broadly, that the world
seems to be telling Dylan that he and the girl are unsuited to
each other, but Dylan disagrees. (Compare the way classical
pastoral elegy has, say, the whole world mourning the death
of Bion.) However, the 'world' is arbitrary, idiosyncratic and
unrecognisably narrow: why is the undertaker guilty? Why is

the organ-grinder lonesome? What is a washed-out horn? You could say that meanings here aren't available to us because Dylan's references are hermetically private. You could say that Dylan was stoned when he wrote it – on acid and on Thomas. Either way, it is nonsense unless, or even if, 'Everybody Must Get Stoned'.

In Andrew Solt's 1996 documentary film *Imagine: John Lennon*, there is footage of an interesting encounter between Lennon and a young man, who has clearly taken drugs and has been sleeping rough in the grounds of Lennon's Tittenhurst Park estate. The young man thinks that, meeting him, Lennon will just 'know'. (By which he means 'know' why he is hanging about, why he wants to talk to Lennon. He thinks Lennon's songs have some special meaning directed at him.) Lennon replies: 'So we met. I'm just a guy. I write songs... Anything fits if you're tripping off some trip... I was just having fun with words. It was literally a nonsense song. *I mean Dylan does that*, anyone does that. You stick 'em together and see if they have any meanings... Some of them do, some of them don't...' [my italics: Lennon was less overawed than Christopher Ricks].

Can pure sound mean anything? A fire alarm? On the Cross-Channel ferry, passengers are told in advance what the alarm sounds like and what it means. The sound itself means nothing. But is music a special case? Can music mean anything, in other words? How misleading that phrase 'in other words' is in this context. Pure music is wordless.

In his *Autobiography*, Stravinsky said that music is incapable of saying anything, incapable of expressing anything except itself: 'music is... powerless to express anything at all: a feeling, an attitude, a psychological state.'

(Stravinsky is right – unless, of course, the composer is setting words. I make a distinction here between music without words and music which sets words – lieder, opera, the oratorio. Dylan's 'I Want You' uses words, words emptied of sense, even though they have 'the sound of sense', in Robert Frost's famous formulation. By 'the sound of sense', Frost meant the *tune* we hear when people are talking, even if we can't hear what they are saying. Frost's example of 'the sound of sense', in a letter to John T. Bartlett (4 July 1913), is the sound, the cadences of speech we hear through a closed door: 'The best place to get the abstract sound of sense is from voices behind a door that cuts off the words.')

Stravinsky's assertion doesn't command instant agreement. Most of us do think music expresses something. Our representative can be the speaker in Browning's 'A Toccata of Galuppi's': 'I can hardly misconceive you; it would prove me deaf and blind; / But *although I take your meaning*, 'tis with such a heavy mind!' [my italics]. He listens and he knows what the composer means. In fact, however, Browning's poem is about the way *we read meaning into the music*. The Venetians hear Galuppi's toccata and it endorses their licentiousness. The speaker hears in the toccata Venetian mortality, a *memento mori*. The toccata induces two completely opposed meanings, releases two competing solipsisms.

Music has no words so it can have no meaning intrinsically. I assume as my premise that meaning is restricted to words. Which may sound too narrow. True, trees aren't meaningful. Birdsong isn't meaningful. (To birds, it means something, but we don't know what or how it means.) But what about tears, say? Can't they mean something? Or a gesture? A gesture of dismissal, of rejection. A blown kiss? Tears depend on context for their meaning. They can be tears of pain (the mote in the eye); tears of sorrow; tears of joy; tears of laughter. Tears in themselves are unresolved. Gestures are also ambiguous – unless they are examples of deaf sign language. In Claude Lanzmann's film *Shoah*, the Polish peasants made throat-slitting gestures to the Jews in the incoming cattle trucks. They intended to warn the Jews of their imminent fate. But the gesture could as easily have been read as simple hatred and hostility (and in some cases probably was). In Marilynne Robinson's novel *Home*, the senile clergyman Reverend Boughton makes a gesture of rejection to his son Jack. Without the novelist's gloss on the gesture, the movement of his hand might mean anything – for example, sudden pain. Even simple expressions can be misleading. Hamlet: 'one may smile, and smile, and be a villain.' Even a scream can be a scream of pleasure, as well as an index of fear. Think of all those teenage girls at Beatles' concerts.

Words themselves, though less crude semantically, aren't entirely unambiguous, of course. But language can be an extraordinary precision tool for conveying meaning. I tell you how to recognise me at a railway station. I will be wearing a single Wellington boot and my other trouser leg will be rolled up to my knee. Crystal clear unless the train debouches a gaggle of freemasons.

Let me return to the idea of meaning in pure music. I heard Anne-Sophie Mutter play the final rondo of Beethoven's Violin Concerto. It was still a rondo, but it was bone dry, bled of expression, perfunctory, emptied of joy – and extremely pathetic *if you knew her husband had just died of cancer*. The music itself, the notes, told you nothing.

When we listen to music, we feel it has a meaning, but we can't quite say what it is. It's there, but out of sight. So it's a bit like being drunk. We have a sense of benign euphoria or boozer's gloom.

Programme music – music imitative of external, non-musical reality – is a special case. Mussorgsky's *Pictures at an*

*Exhibition*, for example. 'The Ballet of the Unhatched Chicks' sounds completely different if you know Mussorgsky's music represents chicks pecking their way out of their shells – it can be a vivid abstract arrangement of notes, or a slightly vulgar mimesis. Plucking strings or pecking shells: take your choice. Robert Craft has pointed out in *Areté* (24, Winter 2007) that Stravinsky's *Abraham and Isaac*, for all its serialism, is 'all programme music. The rapidly repeated note in the clarinet accompanying the words "multiply thy seed" is an exact mimetic illustration. So is the limitation to strings at all references to God, and the employment of four octaves of C-sharps at the dramatic climax marking the revocation of the human sacrifice.' Richard Strauss's *Symphonia Domestica* is proud of its ability to find a musical equivalent of the composer sharpening his pencil. What is decisive is whether the composer discloses or conceals his programme.

To disclose or not disclose? Joyce had the same problem with the Homeric parallels in *Ulysses*. They are important structurally, extraordinarily inventive, but secondary to the surface narrative of Bloom, Molly and Stephen. Joyce didn't want readers to think that the text of his novel was merely a pretext – that the real point was the identification of arcane, hidden treasure under the surface dross. On the other hand, he didn't want readers to miss the parallels. And so, he suppressed the chapter titles – Aeolus, Hades, Proteus – which had accompanied magazine publication. But he allowed the Linati schema, his structural plan, to be released. He was in two minds.

The listener who knows the programme of a piece of music isn't in two minds. The programme occupies the foreground – unless the programme is discovered long after the listener has listened and learned the music as pure music.

Daniel Barenboim was playing the complete cycle of

Beethoven Sonatas in 2008 at the Royal Festival Hall. On Radio 4, he introduced his project by stating that 'music can tell us about our place in the universe. And we shouldn't ignore this crucial fact.' Fact? *Fact*? What is music telling us about our place in the universe? Tell me that. Unless music is a setting of words, what we hear is precise and self-referential. What we feel, however, is likely to be uplifting, aggrandising, melancholy, *vague...*

Why am I telling you about Barenboim? Because for many readers, and some poets, poetry is equally vague, equally immodest. This is Joseph Brodsky's Nobel acceptance speech: 'The one who writes a poem writes it above all because verse writing is an extraordinary acceleration of consciousness, of thinking, *of comprehending the universe*' [my italics].

Is poetry the highest of the arts? Or just the tallest story?

Brodsky is the snake-oil salesman for poetry, fearlessly fibbing, grotesquely grandstanding, talking up poetry, talking down truth. Faking it.

In his essay on Derek Walcott, 'The Sound of the Tide', Brodsky boasts on his friend's behalf (and on his own):

> To put it differently, these poems represent a fusion of two versions of infinity: language and ocean. The common parent of these two elements is, it must be remembered, time. If the theory of evolution, especially that part of it that suggests we all came from the sea, holds any water, then both thematically and stylistically Derek Walcott's poetry is the case of the highest and most logical evolvement of the species.

Walcott himself is given to the gimcrack aphorism. 'Rhyme', he told Tom Payne in the *Telegraph* (22 January 2011), 'is an attempt to reassemble and reaffirm the possibility of paradise. There is a wholeness, a serenity in sounds coupling to form a memory.' As in 'clap' and 'trap'.

In John Updike's *More Matter*, we can read his (reprinted) review of *Watermark*, Brodsky's tribute to Venice. Updike begins by situating Brodsky among the literary grandees, Valéry, Rilke, Eliot, Henry James – writers who are above the marketplace, above academic politicking, beyond 'the general earthbound sensibility'. They are the Lofty Ones who flatter us with their company. At the same time, Updike helplessly notes the limitations of Brodsky's English: 'Brodsky has written *Watermark* in his adopted English, which is adequate to all but the most artful word-carving, the working of an image to the utmost. It is just this kind of carving, however, that interests him. Alas.' Updike notes: 'it is not always easy to follow the ornate curves of his thoughts.'

I am more cynical than Updike. I wonder if we are meant to follow. The genuinely bogus article, the real unreal thing, is quoted by Updike: 'Assuming that beauty is the distribution of life in the fashion most congenial to one's retina, a tear is an acknowledgement of the retina's, as well as the tear's, failure to retain beauty. On the whole, love comes with the speed of light; separation, with that of sound. It is the deterioration of the greater speed to the lesser that moistens one's eye.' This is a fascinating set of sentences – the commonplace idea of love at first sight, gussied up with A-level physics. The impulse is to obfuscate the banal. Because for some people, poetry is a thing you don't quite understand, or don't fully understand.

People like this posturing. They give you the Nobel Prize for it. As if a new element had been added to the Periodic Table – balonium. Brodsky's Nobel Lecture again: 'If what distinguishes us from other members of the animal kingdom is speech, then literature – and poetry in particular, being the highest form of locution – is, to put it bluntly, the goal of our species.' You can have a high valuation of poetry without pretending it is the ultimate purpose of human life – particularly when it has so few actual readers.

I believe that most poets, most good poets, think meaning is more important than boasting. If you get a poem *wrong*, you won't appreciate the *proper business*, those precise effects.

I began this chapter by evoking the kiss between Helen Schlegel and Paul Wilcox in Forster's *Howards End* – 'the poetry of that kiss'. I want to end with some other kisses – more truly poetic, because more accurate.

Here is Chekhov's kiss in 'The Kiss': 'His neck, round which soft fragrant arms had been so lately clasped, seemed to him to be anointed by oil; on his left cheek near his moustache where the unknown had kissed him there was a faint chilly tingling sensation as from peppermint drops...'

Now Chekhov's kiss in 'My Life': 'Looking for a handkerchief to wipe her tears she smiled; we were silent for some time, then I put my arms around her and kissed her, scratching my cheek till it bled with her hatpin as I did it.'

Another Chekhovian kiss in 'The Teacher of Literature':

The blue material slipped on to the floor, and Nikitin took Masha by the other hand. She turned pale, moved her lips, then stepped back from Nikitin and found herself in the corner between the wall and the cupboard... She threw back her head and he kissed her lips, and that the kiss might last longer he put his fingers to her cheeks; and it somehow happened that he found himself in the corner between the cupboard and the wall, and she put her arms around his neck and pressed her head against his chin.

One of Seamus Heaney's Glanmore Sonnets describes his first full sexual encounter with Marie Heaney: her kiss is a 'deliberate kiss'.

This is Thomas Nashe in *The Unfortunate Traveller*: 'Thy lips on mine like cupping glasses claspe, / Let our tongs meete and striue...'

Now, more fastidiously, Robert Herrick's 'Kisses Loathsome':

> Those lips please me which are plac't
> Close, but not too strictly lac't:
> Yielding I wo'd have them; yet
> Not a wimbling Tongue admit

*Wimbling!*

D. H. Lawrence in *The Rainbow* brings us Lydia Brangwen's 'slow insinuation of a kiss' that melts Tom's bones.

This is Monroe Stahr kissing Kathleen in Scott Fitzgerald's *The Last Tycoon*. There are two kisses. The first is on Kathleen's doorstep. They are about to part. They are about to part when it happens that they join: Fitzgerald's account is full of expertise about the accidentals, the contingencies of kissing. Kathleen is actually trying to make out his face in the early evening dark and leans towards him, the momentum of her face entering his gravitational field. He manoeuvres her face with his chin, the better to kiss her. All the time, she is aware of the shape of the house-key in her hand. A bravura passage touched with telling, true prosaic details – the peripheral key and the technical movement of his chin.

In the second kiss, Stahr holds her so tightly a stitch breaks in her dress. A classy, subtle bodice-ripper.

In Forster's *Longest Journey*, Gerald kisses Agnes. It is a brutal kiss, witnessed by Rickie as he returns to retrieve his sandwiches: 'He had drawn the woman on to his knee, was pressing her, with all his strength, against him.' Forster includes a lot of colour – orchestras, lit mountain peaks etc. – but all the poetry here, in the poet's sense, is in the frank brutality.

What do these examples, all taken from prose, tell us about poetry? That poetry, real poetry, is unafraid of the prosaic. The difference between all these kisses and 'the poetry of that kiss' in *Howards End* is that these kisses are recognisable, recognisably different, unmistakably individual, the opposite of vague. You could pick them out in an identity parade. They have been caught in the act. That is why they are so arresting.

# Chapter Two

---

## *Defining a Rat*

What do we mean by 'poetry'? What do we mean by meaning? What do we mean by meaning in poetry?

The other day I was asked by an editor at the *New Statesman* to write an introductory essay setting out the aesthetic principles behind my art criticism – in effect, to make my implicit ideology manifest. To write a manifesto. In *The Bostonians*, Henry James says of his heroine Verena Tarrant that 'she sidestepped the pitfalls that our consistency sets for us'. I hope to do the same. It is not that one sets out to be inconsistent or candidly contradictory, but that an abstract, theoretical exposition of principles is unnecessary for the practice of criticism and also likely to fall short of comprehensiveness. It is easy enough to understand the attraction exerted by a recipe, a formula, a set of instructions on how to assemble (and disassemble) a poem. Who says no to a short-cut? Who says no to a spell that guarantees magic? What may begin as descriptive, however, can too easily become prescriptive – and pointlessly excluding. My position on looking at pictures, by the way, is this: try not to be stupid; look very carefully; be open-minded. Not much of a manifesto.

All theories must have general application within their province. Aristotle's theory of tragedy in the *Poetics* isn't a theory of tragedy. The *Poetics* are incomplete lecture notes, not a finished and comprehensively expounded theory, descriptive not prescriptive. Compare Saussure's *Cours de linguistique générale* which was also constructed from lecture notes. Later readers have attempted to 'complete' Aristotle's thoughts, to make them apply to all tragedies. We are still trying to work out what his 'theory' meant. The *Poetics* are an explanation that needs explaining – theoretical heaven. We like jargon. Catharsis. Inscape. Instress. Dissociation of sensibility. These are our magnetic rocks, hypnotic with difficulty. And then there are those *faux amis* of theory, ordinary words with newly assigned meanings. Like *langue* and *parole*: '*langue*' meaning not simply language but any system of signifiers; '*parole*' not meaning 'word' but utterance in speech or writing.

My theory is really an anti-theory. Everything that is important about art is particular. Why would you want a theory that applied to everything in general, but nothing in particular? Of course, it makes teaching of literature at university a lot lazier – I mean, easier. You only have to remember one thing. Re-reading becomes less of a priority.

What is 'poetry'? The perils of definition can be seen in Dr Johnson's dictionary definition of a net: 'anything made with interstitial vacuities.' I prefer the use of the object-word. 'Net' is better, clearer than any definition. If you don't know what a net is, Johnson's definition won't help because it isn't a description.

And I stand with Matthew Arnold who stoutly refused to define the terms he deployed: 'the grand style', 'high seriousness', 'criticism of life'. He preferred to illustrate, to cite examples, quotations from Homer that exemplified the grand style. Equally, I could cite Dickens. *Hard Times* is a novel which ridicules definition. Characters are introduced with pastiche dictionary definitions: 'Mrs Gradgrind, a little, thin, white, pink-eyed bundle of shawls, of surpassing feebleness, mental and bodily.' The purpose of this patterning is made clear early in the novel. This is Mr Gradgrind in the classroom: 'Girl number twenty [Sissy Jupe]... Give me your definition of a horse.' Sissy comes from the circus, where her father is a horse-breaker, but she is unable to define a horse. The bloodless Bitzer can: 'Quadruped. Graminivorous. Forty teeth, namely twenty-four grinders, four eye-teeth, and twelve incisive. Sheds coat in the spring; in marshy countries, sheds hoofs, too. Hoofs hard, but requiring to be shod with iron. Age known by marks in mouth.' Undeniably impressive but strangely obliterating.

This is A. E. Housman on poetry in a letter to Seymour Adelman (6 May 1926): 'I can no more define poetry than a terrier can define a rat; but he knows a rat when he comes across one...'

And this is Auden on poets: 'Poets are rarely and only incidentally priests or philosophers or party agitators. They are people with a particular interest and skill in handling words in a particular kind of way which is extremely difficult to describe and extremely easy to recognise.' This is in his introduction to *Poems of Freedom*, edited by John Mulgan.

Notice that two practitioners find recognition easy and definition difficult.

A third, T. S. Eliot, settles for a clubman's pragmatism, definition by committee: in *The Use of Poetry and the Use of Criticism*, he writes, 'What is "all poetry"? Everything written in verse which a sufficient number of the best minds have considered to be poetry.' This begs two questions: who decides what is 'sufficient' and what are the 'best' minds?

Perhaps it is easier to say, not what poetry is, but what it aims to do. In *The Use of Poetry*, Eliot quotes T. E. Hulme's *Speculations* with approval:

> There is a general tendency to think that verse means little else than the expression of unsatisfied emotion… The great aim is accurate, precise and definite description. The first thing is to recognise how extraordinarily difficult this is… Language has its own special nature, its own conventions and communal ideas. It is only by a concentrated effort of the mind that you can hold it fixed to your own purpose.

*The great aim is accurate, precise and definite description.* The layman tends not to value mimesis because he can't see the difficulty involved. The theoretician is likely to wonder about the reality that is being imitated. Neo-Kantians maintain the 'reality' is a construct of the perceiving mind – an arrangement of external data. Other theoreticians – Benjamin Lee Whorf and Edward Sapir – think reality is created by language, a hypothesis now completely discredited. Hulme believes something similar to this, but more plausible, related to the *negative* inertia of language: that language has 'its own conventions and communal ideas'. And therefore, the poet has to avoid being written by the language, but must bend the language to his own purpose.

This is Elizabeth Bishop agreeing, in effect, with Eliot and T. E. Hulme, in the *Christian Science Monitor* just before she died in 1979. She was responding, in an interview, to a criticism sometimes levelled at her work: 'Observation is a great joy. Some critics charge that I'm merely a descriptive poet which I don't think is such a bad thing at all if you've done it well.' It isn't the most robust defence – 'which I don't think is such a bad thing at all' – but it's robust enough in its modestly assertive way. A defence of description.

Some insiders – Brodsky for one – want more than this from poetry. They want meaning in the largest sizes – catering, industrial, *universal*. Description, however accurate, strikes them as modest, pinched, meagre. For their journey through life, they want luxury, leg-room, not a seat in economy. Dr Johnson marks the point when poetry began to change its nature from a medium of instruction and explicit moral generalisation. Imlac, in *Rasselas*, pronounces for Johnson: 'The business of a poet is to examine, not the individual, but the species; to remark general properties and large appearances. He does not number the streaks of the tulip…' At the same time, Johnson was writing his great elegy, 'Ode on the Death of Dr Robert Levet', a poem that contravenes this ruling by focusing tenderly on the individual man: 'Obscurely wise, and coarsely kind.' Eight syllables that bring Levet before us.

Paul Valéry in *Analects* wrote: 'Most people have so little of an idea of what poetry is that this constitutes their definition of poetry'. Perhaps it is possible to describe it, without defining it. Maybe one way of saying what poetry might be is saying what it isn't?

In *A Revenge on Life*, David Caute's biography of Joseph Losey, the film-maker, we learn that Dirk Bogarde in *The Servant* refused to carry a string bag containing a cucumber, two melons and a jar of mayonnaise… He knew what was meant. Losey's film of Robin Maugham's novel turns on the homosexual attraction between Bogarde, the servant, and his employer, played by James Fox. The prop was tendentious. The script was by Harold Pinter. Losey, Pinter and Bogarde collaborated again on the film *Accident*, set in Oxford University. In New York, Pinter and Losey gave a press conference for college editors. A reporter from the *Village Voice* described them as 'consummate phonies' – provoked by their response to a routine question asking what the film meant. Pinter said he would answer the question if he knew what was meant by 'meaning'. Losey joined in the 'Trappist ritual', as John Simon called it.

What do we mean by meaning in poetry? The answer to this question has changed in the twentieth century. T. S. Eliot demotes 'meaning' in *The Use of Poetry* (his Charles Eliot Norton lectures delivered at Harvard in 1933): 'The chief use of the "meaning" of a poem, in the ordinary sense, may be... to satisfy one habit of the reader, to keep his mind diverted and quiet, while the poem does its work upon him: much as the imaginary burglar is always provided with a bit of nice meat for the house-dog.' This is very different from Matthew Arnold for whom the doctrine of poetry, its criticism of life, its moral guidance, could replace religion. Meaning, for Arnold, was of the essence. For Eliot, though, meaning is merely the pretext for the text. Which is to say, the value of a poem is not what it means – say, mortality makes the poet sad – but in the treatment of the subject. In *Couples*, John Updike describes a conversation, moving from participant to participant – the *dance* of conversation – as being like a panama hat woven underwater by virgins in Ecuador around a simple, discardable stone. The stone is the ostensible subject, a pretext for the art of conversation.

But Eliot's demotion is disingenuous because it assumes that meaning is not only secondary and disposable, but available and obvious. In the nineteenth century, this might have been true. The meaning of Arnold's 'The Buried Life', for example, isn't difficult to paraphrase. We are unable to express our true selves for two reasons: we are too gripped by externals to access our true inner selves; secondly, our inner selves are occluded from us. This is Arnold's doctrine.

In the twentieth century, the poetic economy altered. Writing about Kipling, the admiring Eliot notes that Kipling's poetry is too easily accessible to suit contemporary taste. It is fatally obvious. And the same could be said of Arnold or of Pope – it isn't difficult, indeed it is too easy, to identify the piece of meat left by the burglar for the house-dog. It's a T-bone steak; it's spare ribs; it's pork fillet. How did this distaste for obvious, available meaning come about? When did it become vulgar?

Is it possible to date the change? Herbert Grierson's two-volume edition of Donne's poetry appeared in 1912. T. S. Eliot wrote about Donne and the metaphysical poets in 1921, reviewing Grierson's *Metaphysical Lyrics and Poems of the Seventeenth Century: Donne to Butler.* Later in his career, Eliot warns that a poet's criticism of another poet is likely to be a covert advocacy of his own programme. Donne was useful to Eliot's predilection for intellectual content, rhythmic sophistication and interpretative difficulty. 'It is not a permanent necessity that poets should be interested in philosophy, or in any other subject. We can only say that it appears likely that poets in our civilisation, as it exists at present, must be *difficult.*' Not that all of Eliot *is* difficult, if you consider 'The *Boston Evening Transcript*', for example. Or 'La figlia che piange'. But he was thinking of the stranger passages in 'Prufrock', of the 1920 quatrain poems, of 'Gerontion'.

Eliot's reading of Donne is very partial. He favours the striking, isolated image: 'A bracelet of bright haire about the bone.' Eliot admired the 'sudden contrast'. It is more sudden, more vehement here than it actually is in Donne's poem, 'The Relique'. Eliot's cropped quotation is like Picasso reworking Velázquez – a takeover bid. In this version, we are given a striking *memento mori.* In Donne's poem, the bright hair is a simple memento of the woman carried to the man's grave. The speaker is still alive, foreseeing his burial and subsequent disinterment – a thought-experiment. The tone isn't grave, however. It is celebratory of an (unusually) celibate relationship, which goes no further than kissing.

Moreover, Eliot's genuine difficulty is very different from Donne's, where explanatory notes are needed (and supplied by Grierson) for obscure contemporary references. Part of the purpose of Eliot's notes to *The Waste Land* may have been to align himself with Donne in Grierson's presentation.

Eliot's was an influential essay and it was succeeded by I. A. Richards's attempt to theorise the study of literature at Cambridge, to establish principles, in the face of scepticism from university historians and classicists. His *Principles of Literary Criticism* was in tandem with *Practical Criticism* – the latter being the study of poetic texts in isolation from their context, an exercise in deprivation. The names of authors, the historical period, were withheld from the students. (Practical criticism is still central to the Cambridge English course. Now it entails the copious and ingenious extraction of complexity, under examination conditions, from the text set by the examiners. Quantity matters. A book-length study by J. H. Prynne of a single Shakespeare sonnet represents the extreme of this critical methodology, which is predicated, fatally, on the assumption that poetry is inexhaustible.)

Then William Empson, a student of Richards, published *Seven Types of Ambiguity*. Dame Helen Gardner, in her Charles Eliot Norton lectures, *In Defence of the Imagination*, rightly complained that Empson had prematurely stalled the reading process, putting it on 'Pause', before the textual information could be resolved. When we read, we encounter ambiguities. This is quite normal. We then eliminate readings that are unhelpful or irrelevant. Reading is an active process, a sifting, a sorting, a setting aside. For example, this is the opening line of Elizabeth Bishop's 'The Bight': 'At low tide like this how sheer the water is.' *Sheer.* I think everyone's first reading of this word would be 'steep' or 'vertiginous', as in the phrase 'a sheer drop'. But this meaning of 'sheer' doesn't make sense in this context. Bishop's second line: 'White, crumbling ribs of marl protrude and glare'. A second reading supplies us with 'sheer' in the sense of 'transparent', as in 'sheer nylons'. We have a choice between 'perpendicular' and 'diaphanous'. And we choose the latter. In Empson, nothing is set aside, every possibility is kept in play – including the impossible. Criticism as Tantalus. Criticism like Tantric sex, endlessly deferred – and a pain in the balls (not that Dame Helen would have put it quite like that).

The end-point of this methodology is Christopher Ricks, a pun-tormented critic sometimes more interested in what has been nearly said by the poet, the phantom connotation, the verbal innuendo, than by the actual words. Reviewing Seamus Heaney's *Field Work* in the *London Review of Books* (8 November 1979), Ricks, ever fleet, suggested that the word 'manners' (in 'A Dream of Jealousy') carried in its semantic undertow the word 'manna' as a kind of shadow contraband. It was there but it wasn't there. He wrote: '*No need* of manna when the actual is marvellous, our conversation

a white picnic tablecloth spread out
Like a book of manners in the wilderness' [my italics].

Of course, it is acute (and typical of Ricks) to hear the phrase 'manna in the wilderness' but it really is a pun surplus to requirements. The 'actual' *isn't* 'marvellous' in this poem, nor is it miraculous: 'the candour of the light dismayed us'. It is a poem about sexual desire and jealousy – not a happy occasion. The folds of the tablecloth are what make it like a book of manners.

'Likewise,' Ricks immediately continued, talking quickly, this time about another poem, 'The Harvest Bow', 'the word "implicated" is consciously innocent in Heaney: implicated, not in wrongdoing, but as the plaiting of the harvest bow.' The implication is there only to be ruled out. 'Heaney', Ricks tells us, 'practises this beneficent sleight throughout the poems.' Does he now? In another poem, Heaney writes 'as if the unquiet founders walked again' and for Ricks 'the faltering sense of "founders" [as a verb] is felt under the feet of the line'. What is the procedure, the methodology here? To notice a pun, notice it is irrelevant, yet explain its 'function' – as a suspect to be eliminated from enquiries.

And deconstruction – the determination to demonstrate that language can always yield *diametrically opposite* meanings – is, as the New Critic Cleanth Brooks pointed out (in the *Exeter College* magazine), merely Empsonian ambiguity writ large.

In between Empson and Ricks and Deconstruction came the New Criticism. Its premise was taken from I. A. Richards – that the poem itself, pure, unencumbered by biographical and historical information, would reveal itself to the attentive critic. But, after Empson, the critical telos had changed, as we can see from Cleanth Brooks's essays in *The Well Wrought Urn* (1947). The essence, the soul of poetry, was ambiguity – and the critic's task was to uncover it. It was reductive to abstract a single meaning from a poem. For Brooks, the idea of paraphrase was a heresy: form and content were inseparable. Metaphysical poetry, with its argumentative complication, responded better to this dogma of indeterminacy than, say, the poetry of Pope and Arnold – which was, accordingly, silently demoted. Whereas Keats's 'Beauty is truth, truth beauty', on the well-wrought urn, was perfect in its gnomic assertion – a Möbius strip made out of words, twisted to avoid the possibility of closure, and enigmatically set within quotation marks.

In his essay 'The Frontiers of Criticism', Eliot reviewed a New Critical reading of 'The Love Song of J. Alfred Prufrock' by John Wain in a collection called *Interpretations*. He was indulgently bemused. But in fact, Eliot himself was at least partially responsible for this turn criticism had taken. In 1933, Eliot stated in *The Use of Poetry* that 'the poem's existence is somewhere between the writer and the reader'. That is, 'what a poem means is as much what it means to others as what it means to the author; and indeed in the course of time a poet may become merely a reader in respect to his own works, forgetting his original meaning – or, without forgetting, merely changing.' The author, then, hasn't a privileged position. All readers are equal. Logically, it is true that the reader's perception of a poem is the reader's perception of the poem. A mother who has lost a child, for example, might value Elizabeth Barrett Browning's 'To a Dead Child' more than a childless woman. A father who has lost a son might value Ben Jonson's 'On My First Sonne' more than an unmarried undergraduate. Human experience, it goes without saying, will alter the impact of any poem, of any literature. But suppose a reader thinks Jonson's poem is about the sun. The tautology I proposed – the reader's perception of a poem is the reader's perception of the poem – depends on the absence of critical debate. Only a stubbornly stupid reader will insist on the validity of that solar reading of the Jonson. I don't think Eliot meant to defend stupid readings of poetry.

What he is actually driving towards is the collaboration of reader and writer in the uncovering of meaning. The meaning of a poem is no longer explicit as it is in Arnold – like a lapel badge at a conference – but implicit, requiring the intervention of the reader, the cooperation of the reader. This is crucial.

In *The New Poetic*, C. K. Stead proposed that modernism and Eliot in particular were writing a new kind of poetry, radically different from the poetry that preceded it. Stead had unearthed a previously ignored shard of Eliot criticism, a note discovered in Harold Monro's *Collected Poems* (1933): 'It is the poet's business to be original, in all that is comprehended in "technique", only so far as is absolutely necessary for saying what he has to say; only so far as is dictated, not by the idea – for there is no idea – but by the nature of that dark embryo within him which gradually takes on the form and speech of a poem.' Seamus Heaney, in his essay 'The Government of the Tongue', embraces, adopts and expounds Stead's theory. On the one hand, he cites three forgotten poets of 1913 as examples of 'a strong horsepower of common-sense meaning': 'this was poetry that made sense, and compared to its candour and decent comprehensibility, *The Waste Land* showed up as a bewildering aberration.' What do we have instead? '*The Waste Land* in Stead's reading is the vindication of a poetry of image, texture and suggestiveness; of inspiration…' Everyone can go along with the idea of inspiration. It is Heaney's final flourish which elicits my dissent: it is '*poetry which writes itself* [my italics].

Karl Stead is resourceful in argument and deploys supporting evidence shrewdly, but I think his conclusions are mistaken. There is no radical rupture with the past in Eliot's poetry, as the essay 'Tradition and the Individual Talent' makes plain:

> We dwell with satisfaction upon the poet's difference from his predecessors, especially his immediate predecessors; we endeavour to find something that can be isolated in order to be enjoyed. Whereas if we approach a poet without this prejudice we shall often find that not only the best, but the most individual parts of his work may be those in which the dead poets, his ancestors, assert their immortality most vigorously.

'The Love Song of J. Alfred Prufrock', once the dazzle of its novelty has faded, seems now a dramatic monologue in the tradition of Browning. The weight-bearing phrase here – that 'dark embryo' – allows Stead to propose a kind of automatic writing, as mysterious to its author as its reader, both of whom are absolved of the task of making sense of the words on the page. *Of saying what the poem means.* This is Jackson Pollock poetry, a verbal happening, an embrace of contingency. Hermeneutics are bypassed, the work of art *is*. And it is true that Eliot, at the end of *The Use of Poetry*, writes of poetry: 'It may make us from time to time a little more aware of the deeper, unnamed feelings which form the substratum of our being to which we rarely penetrate; for our lives are mostly a constant evasion of ourselves, and an evasion of the visible and sensible world.' *The dark embryo. The substratum of our being.* It sounds very radical.

Actually, it is nothing more than a rephrasing and refurbishing of Matthew Arnold's buried life. The critical note to Monro's poems is dramatically phrased but is merely a back-lit account of the way poems are normally written. Apart from Yeats and Ben Jonson, very few poets write out a prose version and then work it up into poetry. The poet listens to his poem, sees what is implicit there, proceeds by hints, changes his mind according to the poem's internal momentum. All poetry involves discovery at the page. Stravinsky said that he composed every day at the piano: 'the fingers are not to be despised, the fingers are great inspirers.' The poet must be able to improvise.

And this, of course, is very different from writing expository prose. In *The Strangest Man*, a biography of the physicist Paul Dirac, its author Graham Farmelo gives us Dirac's distinction between expository prose and poetry. Apparently, he was puzzled by Robert Oppenheimer's hobby of versifying: 'In science, you want to say something nobody knew before, in words everyone can understand. In poetry, you are bound to say something that everybody knows already in words that nobody can understand.' I think he means more than Emily Dickinson's 'Tell the truth, but tell it slant'. He means something closer to Eliot's analogy between that nice piece of meat and the paraphrasable meaning – but without Eliot's appreciation of those poetic effects, of music, of texture, that for Eliot are primary. For Dirac, they are unnecessary packaging.

Poets wishing to describe poetry frequently (and perhaps unnecessarily) differentiate it from prose. W. H. Auden, in *The Poet's Tongue*, cites the old adage that poetry is 'memorable speech'. He also insists that the poet's subject matter is unrestricted: there is no spectrum of subjects ranging from the 'poetic' to the awkwardly prosaic. His central tenet is that poetry differs from prose because it aims at richness, suggestion, semantic penumbra, whereas prose aims at singleness and accuracy. He proposes a spectrum of meaning.

In *What Good Are the Arts?* John Carey advances the idea of language's 'indistinctness' as a virtue: he sees 'indistinctness' not as a failure (as theoreticians commonly argue) but as a brilliant way of engaging the reader as co-creator. You may think this is similar to Auden's semantic penumbra. It is. But Auden's semantic penumbra is a way of distinguishing poetry from prose and Carey's indistinctness is a shared feature of both prose and poetry.

In any case, Auden's distinction between poetry and prose only holds good for expository prose. Think of Virginia Woolf: 'the train lop-eared with smoke'. Think of Joyce: 'the felly harshed against the kerbstone' [the metal wheel rim made a harsh sound against the kerb]. Think of Nabokov: 'the tennis court was a region of great lakes'. Think of Eliot and T. E. Hulme and their shared aim of accurate description in poetry.

Auden's phrase, 'memorable speech', comes from a lecture given by Arthur Quiller-Couch on 26 February 1916 – and it defines 'literature', not poetry exclusively. 'Literature – the written word – is a permanent record of memorable speech.' Quiller-Couch's argument turns on print: literature is memorable, permanent because it's in print form.

Auden is rewriting Quiller-Couch, massaging 'memorable' until it means that poetry appeals to the emotions and the intellect. Which, of course, applies equally to prose. In any case, how can something semantically indistinct be memorable? (The enigmatic lyrics of pop songs are memorable because of the music. Try memorising this quotation from Melvyn Bragg's *A Time to Dance*: 'I thought – if it is possible to think retrospectively simultaneously with thinking actually – I might have thought that I would have preferred you as you had been before.')

If 'memorable' is difficult, 'speech' is even more problematic: Auden claims, arbitrarily, that poetry is like intimate conversation with a friend. The Milton of *Paradise Lost*? Quiller-Couch argues, more reasonably, that, before print, poetry was song, sung speech. Poetry was originally oral. And therefore, this orality survives into printed poetry.

Quiller-Couch's argument sounds more plausible than Auden, but is itself vulnerable. Robert Frost's (early twentieth-century) poetic programme was to introduce speech rhythms into poetry. Were Quiller-Couch diagnostically right, speech rhythms would already be there. And in fact they are, to a degree. Dramatic poetry – Shakespeare, Webster – is necessarily oral, though you might agree with T. S. Eliot that this is only how people might talk *if they spoke poetry*. It is true, too, that some of Donne's poetry is dramatic: 'For God's sake hold your tongue, and let me love' ('The Canonization').

Frost's assumption – his *agenda* – is that poetry before

Frost's 'sound of sense' wasn't speech-based. (It is a large assumption. The plain diction of Wordsworth's *Lyrical Ballads*, for example, marks a prior self-conscious return to 'the real language of men'.) The more representative, more immediate, nineteenth-century poetry of Keats and Tennyson, however, *is* musically based, lyric writing with intense verbal effects, at the opposite pole from speech. For example, the bravura aural haze of Tennyson's *The Princess*: 'The moan of doves in immemorial elms / And murmuring of innumerable bees.' 'The broad ambrosial aisles of lofty lime / Made noise with bees and breeze from end to end.' But if you want speech-based poetry, you look to Browning or Arthur Clough. Frost's programme is a simplification. Nevertheless, there *is* song-based poetry.

If the poetry of Tennyson isn't sung speech, so much for Quiller-Couch's defining opposition between prose and poetry as sung speech. But suppose we leave poetry undefined for the moment: everyone accepts a gender difference, as it were, between prose and poetry, even if poetry can have a moustache and prose come kitted out with supernumerary nipples and sometimes moobs.

Quiller-Couch argues that the difference between prose and poetry is like crossing the border between Devon and Cornwall: there is a shared area between prose and verse before the real landscape differences become apparent. He argues that the difference is metrical. However, he also points out that Edmund Burke's prose can often be scanned as iambic pentameter. Even here there is a grey area. You could equally cite *Bleak House* where, on the death of Jo the crossing sweeper, Dickens ascends to iambic verse for extended periods.

In any case, isn't the prose poem a problem? Not if you properly understand the status of the prose poem. It doesn't entail a heightened lexis. The prose poem is a piece of prose too short to be an essay or even a very short short story. In German, the prose poem has none of this ambiguity because it is called *eine kleine Prosa*. Perhaps some of Lydia Davis's short stories, given their exceptional brevity, should be classified as prose poems.

It is true, too, that some free verse has no rhythmic pulse and that syllabic verse is defined as being ametrical (a harder condition to contrive than you might imagine. Just think how easily Burke and Dickens stray into metre). So it looks as if rhythm is an inadequate defining principle. However, I would argue that all good free verse has a rhythmic pulse, even Walt Whitman: 'I do not say these things for a dollar or to fill up the time while I wait for a boat.' This long line (twenty monosyllables, apart from 'dollar') looks arhythmical, but it ends with four anapaests, starting with 'or to fill': 'up the time'; 'while I wait'; 'for a boat'. In other words, prose may unconsciously fall into metre, but poetry is always conscious of its presence or deliberate absence. And syllabic verse? Syllabic verse is the conscious repression of rhythm. Rhythm is the absent presence in syllabic verse.

In Auden's view, poetry can address any subject matter, not just elevated subject matter. His implication here is that poetry is often wrongly seen as a special aesthetic, a higher aesthetic, dealing with subjects that lend themselves to poetic treatment – the moon, as it were, rather than the Night Mail. In his essay 'On Poetry in General' (in *Lectures on the English Poets*, 1818), William Hazlitt argues against this catholic attitude to subject matter, maintaining that some bits of life are unauthored poetry – what you might call the intrinsically poetic. Poetry, he avers, is 'not a branch of authorship'. It is a natural condition. I merely cite Hazlitt.

Hazlitt's examples, however, are surprisingly various and include the unpleasant and the nasty. For example, hatred, contempt, miserliness – which aligns him with Auden. The idea of a restricted pool of poetic subjects sits comfortably with the concept of 'poetic diction' in the eighteenth century. It came out of this mind-set, this idea that some subjects were more poetic than others. Wordsworth, in his preface to *Lyrical Ballads*, was quick to subvert poetic diction and embrace the language of real men. He believed poetry should be more prosaic, that prose and poetry shared extensive common ground – that in their language there was no difference. Moreover, for Wordsworth, subject matter was illegitimate as a way of distinguishing between poetry and prose. Wordsworth's subjects were provocatively prosaic – like his lexis – and included an exemplary idiot boy.

Where does that leave us? It leaves us with rhythm, the importance of meaning in poetry, and a 'gender' distinction between poetry and prose. It leaves us with A. E. Housman. 'I can no more define poetry than a terrier can define a rat; but he knows a rat when he comes across one...' Which is more or less where we started.

# Chapter Three

## *Rhythm*

Flaubert, in a letter about *Madame Bovary*, claimed to hear in advance the cadence before he had formulated the precise words. I detect the great novelist placing a shameless advertisement for posterity about his super-normal powers. Flaubert? Self-promotion? Surely not? Think of Norman Mailer's *Advertisements for Myself*. Or Whitman's *Song of Myself*.

The hero of Nicholson Baker's 2009 novel *The Anthologist* is called Paul Chowder. He is editing an anthology of rhyming poetry but is unable to begin the introduction. We learn from Chowder that Allen Ginsberg attacked 'the bad iambic rhythm' in the course of a talk at Naropa Institute, where he was teaching. 'Somebody at the Naropa Institute said, Well then, tell us, Allen. What is the real rhythm of poetry? And Ginsberg replied that the rhythm of poetry was the rhythm of the body. He said that it was, quote, "jacking off under bridges".'

The real rhythm of poetry is not 'jacking off under bridges' because there is no single 'real' rhythm in poetry. There are many rhythms. I include metre under the heading of rhythm because rhythm means a repeated sound pattern of stress.

Repeat. Rhythm means a repeated sound pattern of stress.

So, iambic and trochaic are an alternating pattern of stress. Either te-tum or tum-te. Anapaests (te-te-tum) and dactyls (tum-te-te) are patterns which can be used instead of or in combination with iambs or trochees. Free verse generally has a rhythmic pulse of a less regular kind. Sprung rhythm is a stress-based poetry with a given regular pattern of stresses and an undetermined number of unstressed syllables. Gerard Manley Hopkins's example of sprung rhythm is the three-stress in the first line of 'Ding dong bell'. The second line is 'Pussy's in the well' where the stress falls on *Puss, in* and *well*. Thereafter, the pattern of stresses is maintained. *Who put* him *in? Little Tommy Tin.*

The ability to scan has disappeared into some witness protection programme. It has been given a new identity. In its place we have the protectively imprecise idea of 'rhythms'. Where there used to be Mr Scansion pedantically counting the buttons on his waistcoat, there is now Jo Rhythms laid-back in a unisex floating kaftan. Let's not get heavy, hey. Rhythm? Whatever.

When scansion does make a brief comeback, its features are often subtly different. The familiar face seems unchanged yet its expression is anxious. This is because it has gone profoundly deaf. Terry Eagleton, in *How to Read Literature* (2013), tells his readers that the first line of Larkin's 'The Whitsun Weddings' is 'an iambic pentameter', 'calculatedly flat, casual and colloquial'. This is the first line: 'That Whitsun, I was late getting away'. It has ten syllables but it is not an iambic pentameter, not even a 'calculatedly flat' one. The penultimate foot, 'getting', is an emphatic trochee. Before that, it is a strain to assimilate the line to the iambic pentameter template. 'Getting' does for the iambic project definitively.

Jonathan Bate, in the foreword to the *Cambridge Companion to Creative Writing*, says that scansion is no longer taught at universities:

> University degrees in music [and art]... have an emphasis
> on technique and on practice that is rarely encountered

within a traditional English degree... It is not usually demanded of literature students that they should be skilled in the literary equivalents of such techniques as playing a scale, composing a variation, sketching a nude: they are not habitually asked *to scan a line of verse*, compose a sonnet... [my italics]

Maybe this is why Sean O'Brien, a graduate of the Cambridge English tripos, should have baffled Brian Jones many years ago. Jones wrote in the *London Magazine*:

In Sean O'Brien's poetry, I find a strange obliviousness to craft which becomes intrusive and disabling. Can it be possible that a poet can start a poem with the line
    Consoled by the dead and their tea-things
and not be aware that the rhythm he is so strongly establishing is precisely that of
    The sexual life of a camel
and other verses more or less scurrilous? Or begin another with
    You've been leaving for years and now no one's surprised
    When you knock to come in from the weather
and not be prepared to acknowledge, or use for effect in the rest of the poem, the rhythms of Gilbert's nightmare patter-song, where you dream you are on a steamer from Harwich
    Which is something between a large bathing machine
    And a very small second-class carriage?
A poet may, of course, use any form he wishes for any purpose, but O'Brien does not seem aware of the rhythmical expectations he sets up, or the ways they might affect the reader. The lines with which the two poems I quote con-

tinue have no clear metrical values, and I suspect this is not a deliberate or ironic act on O'Brien's part, but the result of inattention or of lack of concern.

The universities...

Twenty years ago, I discussed with a professor at the Universidad Autonóma, Madrid, his research project, 'The Rhythm of Modernism' – as if Modernism had a unique rhythm that distinguished it from all previous rhythms. He was promising to discover Modernism's rhythmic PIN. So much for, say, the basically iambic metre of Eliot's 'The Love Song of J. Alfred Prufrock': 'My morning coat, my collar mounting firmly to the chin'. Or Auden's catalectic trochaics in 'Now the leaves are falling fast, / Nurse's flowers will not last, / Nurses to their graves are gone, / But the prams go rolling on.' Not to mention Auden's 'Night Mail' with its virtuoso mimesis of the steam engine's changing rhythm: 'This is the Night Mail crossing the border' (dactyl, trochee, dactyl, trochee: 'Mail' doesn't take a stress, counter-intuitively, in this line); 'Letters of thanks, letters from banks' (trochee, iamb, trochee, iamb). The research came to nothing.

A point of interest in Nicholson Baker's novel *The Anthologist* is whether Baker shares his protagonist's rhythmic theories. Chowder thinks there is one real rhythm: 'The real rhythm of poetry is a strolling rhythm. Or a dancing rhythm.' Then Chowder quotes and mis-scans Edna St Vincent Millay's 'Love has gone and left me and I don't know what to do'. Her seven-beat trochaic septameter catalectic is said to have four beats only. He continues by mis-scanning A. A. Milne and Thomas Bailey Aldrich, T. S. Eliot and Edgar Allan Poe. As for the Poe, he quotes John Frederick Nims on its scansion – a 'trochaic octameter with lines two and four catalectic', which is exactly right

– and dismisses him: 'And how far does that get you? It actually disables any understanding of the poem to say that what he's doing is trochaic octameter. Because it's still really a basic four-beat stanza.' It isn't.

Poets aren't guiltless either in their accounts of how their poems come to be written – and the mysterious role of rhythm in the process. In essence, the consensus is that the poem first makes itself felt as the fugitive presence of a unique rhythm, haunting the ear. Hopkins in a letter to Canon R. W. Dixon (5 October 1878) tells how he started 'The Wreck of the Deutschland': 'I had long had haunting my ear the echo of a new rhythm which now I realised on paper. To speak shortly, it consists in scanning by accents or stresses alone, without any account of the number of syllables...' Fair enough in the special case of Hopkins whose rhythms are genuinely innovatory, but the fugitive rhythm can hardly apply to his predecessors whose metres were standard, not fugitive at all. Milton and Pope, say, can hardly have started by the need to realise the iambic metre on paper. For Dryden and Swift, writing poetry wasn't a branch of psychical research.

It begins in the twentieth century. You can find the concept in Scott Fitzgerald's *The Great Gatsby* where it is a heightened version of that elusive something at the tip of your tongue, at the edge of consciousness, out of the corner of your eye, within the blind-spot. Gatsby is talking high-flown romantic nonsense about, for example, tuning forks and stars (a version of the music of the spheres). The dry, sceptic narrator Nick Carraway deplores his sentimentality yet locates a fugitive truth he finds it difficult to put into words. The words are there at the very edge of consciousness, a reminiscent rhythm which is finally elusive. But the ertsatz intuition caves to rotting.

*Fitzgerald knew what an unreliable prompt that elusive rhythm is.*

In poetry, the idea begins with Paul Valéry, who, as always, resists obfuscation and mystery. (On Victor Hugo: 'The very qualities which Hugo thought would make him immeasurably great and rank him with the gods merely make him seem ridiculous. His notion was based on a fallacy. A poet should make no secret of his calling, own up to his midnight oil, and not profess to hear mysterious voices.' Ruefully, though, Valéry concludes: 'But would people have any use for poetry if it did not claim to be oracular?')

This is Valéry's account of the composition of 'Le cimetière marin':

> my intention was at first no more than a rhythmic figure, empty and filled with meaningless syllables, which obsessed me for some time. I noticed this figure was decasyllabic, and I pondered on that model which is very little used in modern French poetry; it struck me as poor and monotonous, of little worth compared with the alexandrine... The demon of generalisation prompted me to try raising this Ten to the power of Twelve.

He begins with a *precise* rhythmic figure, a decasyllabic line.

Watch as other poets gradually assimilate this cogent process to the oracular, the Delphic, the semi-divine.

T. S. Eliot, in 'The Music of Poetry' (1942), writes, following Valéry: 'I know that a poem, or a passage of a poem, may tend to realise itself first as a particular rhythm before it reaches expression in words, and that this rhythm may bring to birth the idea and the image; and I do not believe this is an experience peculiar to myself.' Indeed not. Eliot had Valéry to back him up.

After Eliot, poets are queuing to own up to their oracular powers and their irresistible musical imaginations, to their rhythmic categorical imperatives. Here are some poets stuck in the stationary queue – stationary because it is going nowhere.

Richard Murphy in *Viewpoints: Poets in Conversation with John Haffenden* (1981): 'In fact, when I was writing "The Last Galway Hooker", I derived the rhythm of the poem to some extent from *Gawain and the Green Knight* as well as directly from the sea, the rhythm of the waves.' *The rhythm of the waves.* You want to hoot like D. H. Lawrence chortling over Whitman's 'I am he that aches with amorous love' – '*Chuff*, Walt!'

The rhythm of the waves. Is that Dylan Thomas's sea 'tumbling in harness'? Or singing 'in its chains'? Or is it Alice Oswald's trochaic sea in *Memorial*, which 'lifted and flattened lifted and flattened'? Tell it to the marines. Tell it to the marine.

Geoffrey Hill in *Viewpoints* gives a rather more plausibly intricate account of inspiration (aka frustration in Hill's case) which nevertheless draws as much on Eliot's template in 'The Music of Poetry' as actual experience:

I've gone sometimes for ten years knowing – in a curiously precise way – that something is waiting to be written; the only obstacle is a total inability to write it. It would be too fanciful to call it a Platonic shape, but I can't think of any other way of describing that strange mixture of nagging and calming allurement – sometimes clear, sometimes hazy, but definitely unattainable for the time being. Then, if I'm lucky, various germinal phrases or *a hint of rhythm* or something as minutely technical as the cadence of an enjambement will begin to stir... Such phrases and rhythms and cadences are ganglions in which intellect and emotion and the minute necessary technical adjustments are held together in some way that one knows is full of possibility. [my italics]

Anne Stevenson began as a musician and takes her place on the bandwagon, listening to the pianissimo rhythmic husk. Appearing on Radio 4's *Front Row* (14 November 2007), she was asked how her poems began, and replied that it was usually a fugitive rhythm...

In *Poetry* (March 2007), she came to the cliché afresh: 'Although I rarely write in set forms now, poems still come to me as tunes in the head. Words fall into rhythms before they make sense. It often happens that I discover what a poem is about through a process of listening to what its rhythms are telling me.'

Alfred Hickling reported something similar, but not identical, in 'Border Crossings', a profile in *The Guardian* (2 October 2007): 'Stevenson says that "almost always it is some overheard musical rhythm or phrase which sets me writing", and, until her late teens, she assumed that she was destined to be a musician rather than a poet.'

On 14 December 2007, she was telling *The Times* and Tom Gatti that she had studied the cello for two years at the University of Michigan before deciding that she would never be a first-rate cellist. However, music remained the springboard and the backbone of her verse, 'the sound leading the hand', as she puts it in her dialogue poem 'Making Poetry'.

This is Fleur Adcock's characteristically modest and downbeat version of the rhythmic *ignis fatuus*: 'in my own writing I'm always conscious of the rhythm, without always being in control of it; quite often my feeling is that a poem is being dictated to me, rather than by me, particularly in the early stages...' (from 'Not Quite a Statement' in *Strong Words*). This is less vulnerable to mockery than Richard Murphy because Fleur Adcock prefers free verse and is lucid about the difficulties of free verse. There is no given measure. The ear judges. 'Free verse seems to me the purest type of verse, in that its rhythms are entirely innate and inherent in phrases that make it up. It has no rules by which to adjust them. I find it extremely difficult to write.' Which is why she has to listen to the rhythm of the phrase that 'arrives' in her head. This seems to me a truer account than most about the way poems begin – with a phrase and its cadence, and not with a disembodied rhythm wandering the maze of the ear looking for its lost words.

William Carlos Williams seems to me nearly right when he complains in 'On Measure – Statement for Cid Corman' (1954) that the old measure has gone and that we need a new measure. 'We have no measure by which to guide ourselves except a purely intuitive one which we feel but do not name.' He is ruling out a return to metre – perhaps too dogmatically, since, as Eliot long since pointed out, in his essay 'Reflections on Vers Libre', the best free verse is always flirting with metre. On the other hand, look how few academics can scan.

One last example of a rhythm arriving in a poet's ear – this time an instance that makes perfect sense and isn't pretending to aural arcana. On 11 July 2012, James Fenton was talking to Mark Lawson on *Front Row*. Fenton explained that, as he was storming the palace of President Marcos in the Philippines, a line of poetry came to him with a particular pronounced rhythm and he adjured himself not to forget it in the excitement of politics. The line became part of his poem 'Here Come the Drum Majorettes': 'There's a girl with a fistful of fingers.' Fenton glossed the rhythm: 'de-de-**duh duh** de-de-**duh**-de.' Which, funnily enough, isn't quite right. The line is an anapaest, an anapaest, an anapaest, and a hypermetric foot (an extra syllable). The point is, though, that Fenton wasn't visited by anything previously unheard.

I like Auden's line about Rimbaud: 'Verse was a special illness of the ear.' Poets have to pay attention to the pain, listen until the line gets better. We take the phrase that arrives in our ear – and we fix it, try it this way, try it that way, until we feel a perfect fit.

Of course, rhythm, the rhythm section, of any poem is only a section. Other ingredients include rhyme, metaphor, diction, stanza form. Sometimes the proportions vary. Depending on circumstances, there will be more of one because there is less of another. When I wrote the songs for *The Electrification of the Soviet Union*, my libretto for Nigel Osborne's opera, realism demanded my characters have less metaphor than I usually had recourse to. I found that rhyme was needed as a kind of compensation for the muted metaphorical resource.

Similarly, Paul Muldoon's poetry is rhythmically muted, its pulse practically non-existent, because the rhyming is so extensive and rich. In 'The Man and the Echo', Yeats asks: 'Did that play of mine send out / Certain men the English shot?' Muldoon guys this in his pastiche, in *7, Middagh Street*, of Yeats's tetrameter couplets in 'Under Ben Bulben' – 'If Yeats had saved his pencil-lead / would certain men have stayed in bed?' This is almost shocking, certainly striking, in a poetic economy where rhyme, not rhythm, is the central engine. In '[Vico]' from *Madoc*, for example, Muldoon illustrates Vico's idea of a circular temporal continuum, not only by the Escher-like end that takes us to the squirrel at the very beginning – but also by the mirror rhyme scheme. The first three lines 'rhyme' with the last three lines: 'A hand-wringing, small grey squirrel / plods / along a wicker' is inverted in the last three, 'to a wicker / treadmill in which there plods / a hand-wringing, small grey squirrel'. This pattern is reproduced through the poem. The fourth line ends with the word 'attached', so the fourth line from the conclusion ends with 'rachets'. The distance between the rhymes diminishes. At the poem's centre, there is the couplet: 'and spindles // and tappets and trundles'.

# Chapter Four

## *The Line*

Hopkins, discussing his invention of sprung rhythm, denies Whitman co-authorship even though he admits there are lines of sprung rhythm in Whitman. These lines are merely unconscious – accidents of Whitman's approximate, intuitive prosody. To be a practitioner of sprung rhythm, Hopkins argues, you have to *know* what you are doing. You have to be self-conscious. To apply for a patent, you need to know what is new and be able to describe it, distinguishing it from other inventions in the field.

The same thing applies to the poetic line. Every serious poet has to have thought about it. And you would have thought most have. The poetry world, however, prizes its subjectivity, its intuition, the escape from arithmetic into irrefutability and the appeal to the infallible ear – which often proves to be tin.

Notoriously, poetry doesn't go to the margins. We can all agree about that. Cadence and sense are interdependent. Can we agree about that? It is difficult to have a cadence that runs counter to sense: 'Funny how / people pick / their noses' is a stanza from Robert Creeley's 'Hotel Lobby'. 'Funny how' is not a cadence. Nor is it sense.

(I make an exception for William Carlos Williams's 'The Red Wheelbarrow':

so much depends
upon

a red wheel
barrow

glazed with rain
water

beside the white
chickens

'Beside the white' is not a cadence, or a unit of sense. It doesn't matter. This is a concrete poem, whose form is a *carmen figuratum*, a shaped song, like Herbert's 'Easter Wings', which are shaped like wings. William Carlos Williams's stanzas are little mimetic wheelbarrows.)

The line is the fundamental unit of poetry. And the concept of the line as a unit, therefore, has important implications for the line-break. What is the line? Can it be described and fixed? Or is it various?

Obviously, it is various: the trochaic dimeter is a line of four syllables; an iambic tetrameter a line of eight syllables divided into four metric feet; the iambic pentameter a line of ten syllables divided into five feet. So, various. Yet consider some of Joseph Brodsky's deplorable line-breaks – maladroit because serving not the line, but the rhyme scheme. Some examples taken from his last collection, *So Forth* (1996): in the title poem, Brodsky evokes autumn via grouse-shooting and the rhyme-word is 'double-barrel': 'you'll cock up your double-barrel, / but to inhale more oxygen rather than to imperil / *grouse.*'[my italics] In 'Centaurs I', we encounter the same one-word leftover remnants:

A winter evening,
tired of its eye-batting blueness, fondles
like a witless atom on the eve of being
split the remaining hours' golden
*chain*. [my italics and this violation of the line for the
dubious 'fondles' 'golden' rhyme]

Later in the same poem 'wanly' rhymes with 'only' and produces this 'line': 'since there's nothing they can turn themselves
into. Only'. This is a stanza from 'Clouds':

heeding? To whose
might do you yield?
Or
who is your builder?
Your Sisyphus?

The contrived rhymes ('builder'–'yield or', 'whose'–'Sisyphus')
result in poetic Thalidomide. It is impossible to read without
feeling the awkwardness.

In other words, the line is manifestly various, but for all its
varieties there is an overarching concept of the line. Which is
that the poetic line should be a unit of sense. If this is the given,
the assumed template, then variants of the template will be conscious decisions – meaningful because of the template.

Another sexual analogy. There are many kinds of sex. But
we also have the idea of perversity – of abnormal sex. For
many people, the sexual power of the perverse act is located
in the violation of the 'normal'. Think of the counter-intuitive
line-break as pleasurable perversity – against the natural grain.
There has to be a sense of the normal line as fundamental, as a
given that validates the variant.

In much American poetry, this violation is so universal that it is no longer perverse, no longer meaningful. In, say, Sharon Olds or Anne Carson, the line-breaks are always counter-rational – to distinguish poetry from prose.

In England, we have a comic version of this procedure with Barry Fantoni's inept amateur poet, E. J. Thribb, whose poems on public figures are published in *Private Eye*. Thus 'Lines on the Return to Britain of Billy Graham', where the lines are counter-intuitive:

> Keith and I
> Have terrific arguments
> About religion.
>
> My view is
> Far too complicated
> To explain in a
> Poem.

The first stanza quoted here is prosaic and without rhythm, but its lines are rational units – inelegant, abrupt but just possible. The final stanza is chopped up with spectacular disregard for sense: 'To explain in a'. (There is a paradox here, which is that these inept line-breaks are, given their comic purpose, perfect line-breaks. They are perfectly imperfect, exactly inexact. They are consciously engineered.)

Sharon Olds's poem 'The Connoisseuse of Slugs' examines the similarities between an erection and the horns of a slug. Of its twenty-two lines, three end with the word 'the' and one with the word 'its'. You might argue that the definite article at the end of the line creates suspense: the *what*? However, if the word is ordinary and doesn't justify the suspense ('odor', 'sensitive'), the effect is misleading. In any case, this 'effect' shouldn't be repeated three times in the same poem. It looks technically impoverished. Actually, there is no technique whatsoever.

Anne Carson's 'Irony is not Enough: Essay on my Life as Catherine Deneuve' was published in the *Seneca Review* in 1997. It is about a woman teacher's erotic fascination with a female pupil. This is an extract from Section XI, *Snows*:

> The woman feels like
> something hooked
> or washing out to sea, but the force of life coming off
> this girl
>
> is too strong
> to think what
> day it is or what was supposed to happen. Dusk
> reaches
>
> them.
> She switches on
> the desklamp. But now the girl is lifting her coat...

I want to be as fair as possible to Anne Carson, who has many other virtues as a writer. So, I think you could justify the linear confusion of 'to think what / 'day it is or what was supposed to happen...' After all, the speaker is discombobulated by infatuation. The oddness of 'to think what / day it is...' is arguably a mimetic line-break. And the three-line stanzas overall are written to a template of two short lines and a long line. Carson is thinking about shape.

But there is no justification for the stanza-break, not just a line-break, between 'Dusk reaches // them'. 'Them' is difficult to justify as a line. One-word lines are not impossible, but they are rarely successful. Seamus Heaney's 'Kinship' manages two words in two consecutive lines: 'But *bog* / meaning soft...' The word 'bog', unlike the word 'them', is central and significant since Heaney's sequence is a sequence of bog poems, paralleling Danish ritual sacrifice and contemporary Ireland during the Troubles.

This is Anne Carson again. The girl is wearing:

a new

silver

earring. *Thank you*, she says after the girl translates.

Even if we invoke some dazed, stunned, stoned, near catatonic inner state – brought about by the thunderbolt of Passion – the lines about the earring are too like the product of skilful speech therapy on a stroke patient. That sensation of slow-motion perception and hearing is too like the dying man in a movie trying to tell us where the treasure is buried – and failing. Master Patrick Dignam, in *Ulysses*, remembering his dying father: 'I couldn't hear the other things he said but I saw his tongue and his teeth trying to say it better.'

We are actually in the presence of the arbitrary. There is no mimesis. There is no reason. On 30 September 2013, Anne Carson was on Radio 4's *Start the Week*, talking to Stephanie Flanders about her latest book *Red Doc*, which is arranged in two-inch-wide columns:

I wish I could say it was conscious. No, I was messing around on the computer with the format features and one day the whole text shrank to this column and it looked so great I just left it. But interestingly I had to rewrite the text because having those units of meaning on the page in that little channel made the rhythms work differently and it found its own proper rhythm. Also I was able to succeed in my original project of writing a whole novel with only one comma... [Previously] It had a play version, it had an actual screenplay version, it had a total verse version, a total prose version and they were all completely awful and then the computer did this channel in the middle of the page and it became clearer... You have to trust John Cage more and go with that impulse.

It may sound radical to invoke Cage and stuffy to object to this arbitrary procedure – a bit like faulting Jackson Pollock's drip paintings. But the line is the fundamental unit of poetry. The line is the steering wheel that harnesses the Pegasus-power of poetry. You can't give up the steering wheel, you can't relinquish control. And actually Anne Carson doesn't concede control completely: the format involves rewriting. We don't know how much. (As for Pollock, I'm with Giacometti, who characterised Abstract Expressionism as 'l'art du mouchoir'.)

It is hard (for me) to read these lines from Geoffrey Hill's holocaust poem 'September Song' without the aural doppel-gänger of E. J. Thribb making his ghostly, ghastly presence felt:

> (I have made
> an elegy for myself it
> is true)

To be sure: 'To explain in a.'

When he is writing unrhymed poetry, Hill's line-breaks are more like tics than decisions – like those addictive red dots on the paintings of William Coldstream. He favours the solitary word at the end of a line, isolated, cut off by punctuation. Irres-istibly reminding you of a word on a high ledge, wanting to be talked down by the police: 'The *Venice* portrait: he / Broods, the achieved guest'; 'Virtue is virtù. These / Lips debate'; 'But few appearances are like this. Once / Every five hundred years a comet's'. None of these examples is more than a mannerism. They serve no other purpose.

Now Seamus Heaney's exemplary 'Funeral Rites':

> They had been laid out
>
> in tainted rooms,
> their eyelids glistening,
> their dough-white hands
> shackled in rosary beads.

You can hear that every line is a rational unit, both a cadence and a unit of sense. Reviewing *North*, Edna Longley said that Heaney's short lines were merely divided iambic pentameters, which was her way of telling potential readers that Heaney's short lines were in fact nothing new. It is palpably not the case that these lines are iambic. Near pentameters perhaps, but not iambic.

(Heaney isn't infallible. From the same poem, 'Funeral Rites':

> the flames hovering
> to the women hovering
>
> behind me.

That 'behind me' looks a little lost, cut off from its syntactical companions across a stanza-break, a little vulnerable and insub-stantial.)

The long line is as difficult to manage as the short line, if not more so. C. K. Williams's *Flesh and Blood* has some interesting attempts to use the long line as a way of capturing the speaking voice and its momentum – the way its momentum is naturally longer than the usual poetic line. 'Reading: The Cop':

> Usually a large-caliber, dull-black, stockless machine gun
>     hangs from a sling at his hip
> where a heavily laden cartridge belt in the same blue as his
>     special-forces uniform cinches his waist,
> and usually he stands directly in the doorway, so that
>     people have to edge their way around him –
> there was some sort of bombing in the building, and pre-
>     sumably this is part of his function.
> He often seems ill at ease and seems to want to have but
>     doesn't quite because he's so young
> that menacingly vacant expression policemen assume
>     when they're unsure of themselves or lonely…

This is less Whitman than Frost – the Frost who was mesmerised by actual speech, who recorded in his poem 'New Hampshire' this parenthetic redundancy, '(You won't believe she said it, but she said it)'. Williams is after the way we anchor our speech with repetition ('usually', twice), the way we introduce parenthetical thought that interrupts the completion of our sentences. Williams *knows* he is writing counter to the line. His policeman 'seems to want to have… that menacingly vacant expression', but Williams splices in a digressive pre-emptive qualification: 'but doesn't quite because he's so young.'

This extract has six lines. The first line is twenty-two syllables. The other lines are comparably long. To read this aloud, you need to take a run at it. You need to know where the sense is going – but the impetus begins to tie up badly in the fifth and sixth lines where there are ellipses. The lactic acid gets to the muscles.

The cop is reading something Williams thinks might be a political pamphlet. The last line is very funny, a snook-cocking, anti-plangent line, of stuttering comedy: 'I was curious and thought I'd just stop, go back, peek in, but then I thought, no, not.'

This radical denial of the conventional poetic line – Williams's lines go to the margins and beyond – is really difficult to bring off. From James Fenton's 'A German Requiem' you learn a more reliable way of managing the longer line – by the use of candid rhetoric, the bold repetitions, the marked caesurae, the polarised structures of denial and assertion:

It is not what they built. It is what they knocked down.
It is not the houses. It is the spaces between the houses.
It is not the streets that exist. It is the streets that no longer
    exist.

The emphatic caesurae bring to mind Miroslav Holub's thoughts on the line as a poetic unit in his title essay 'The Dimension of the Present Moment': drawing on the research of F. Turner and E. Pöppel (Holub was a scientist as well as a poet), Holub floats the hypothesis that lines, successful, classic lines, when read aloud, take from two to three seconds. Longer lines divide into two sections of three seconds. 'Greek and Latin epic hexameters are divided by a strong caesura into two three-second segments. Shorter lines are read with marked pauses.' (There is a serious difficulty here for Holub's thesis: it is that the placing of classical Latin caesurae is consciously varied.) In sum, 'the three-second poetic LINE of Turner and Pöppel appears to be a

"carrier-wave" of traditional poetries in any language system.'
Holub did a little personal back-up research: on Czech TV he
listened to poems by Nezval and 'a line lasted almost exactly
three seconds, shorter lines were prolonged by slower reading
or pauses, longer ones were reduced by a quicker tempo. I was
almost frightened...'

You don't have to accept these dimensions as sacrosanct. But
think about those short lines of Heaney and how they sound in
your head, how, even in the context of short lines, their dramatic shortness *gives you pause*:

> But *bog*
> meaning soft.

There is no question. The length of the line is deliberate, inviting us to deliberation.

Ciaran Carson's 'Cocktails' is a poem about tall stories concerning the Troubles in Northern Ireland. Carson is taking off
from the example of C. K. Williams. In this poem, the template
of the line is overridden with four enjambed lines, the better to
arrive at a pronounced pause:

> Bombing at about ninety miles an hour with the exhaust
>     skittering
> The skid-marked pitted tarmac of Kennedy Way, they hit
>     the ramp and sailed
> Clean over the red-and-white guillotine of the check-point
>     and landed
> On the M1 flyover, then disappeared before the Brits knew
>     what hit them. So
> The story went...

The momentum is mimetic. The effect is crude but effective.

The point is this. Hans Keller, the musicologist, told me that pattern in music is unimportant. *Disruption* of the pattern is musically important. You can illustrate this with metre quite easily. If you set up the expectation of an iambic pentameter, then an irregularity in the centre of the line is significant. Wordsworth's *Prelude* (Book II): 'She seemed with difficult steps to force her way.' This line doesn't have ten syllables but eleven. The extra syllable is in the word 'difficult'. The difficulty is in the word 'difficult': to scan the line regularly, 'difficult' has to be bi-syllabic, 'diff'cult'. Only a variant in the middle of the line counts as significant. The first metric foot can be inverted – a trochee instead of an iamb – and the rules can accommodate a hypermetric extra beat at the line's end.

It is important to know the rules of scansion. They are a significant tool for achieving very precise effects. Many academics and some poets (Glyn Maxwell, Michael Hofmann, by their own admission) are unable to scan. Essentially, you apply a rhythmic template, established in the first line, to the subsequent lines. The iambic pentameter means five feet, each of which is a de-dum. This is always approximate and depends on joined-up listening – an overall feel for rhythm, not the analysis of each individual syllable. For example, it is possible in a metric line that an unimportant word like 'the' will take a stress, while a relatively important word does not. For example: in Donne's 'Go, and Catch a Falling Star', the overall template means that, in this line, a trochaic tetrameter, the word 'that' takes a stress while the word 'strange' does not: 'All strange wonders that befell thee.' If the template cannot be comfortably imposed, you then have a significant variant. From the same poem – 'Till age snow white hairs on thee' – which takes stresses on every syllable except 'on'. A trained, experienced ear will distinguish between allowable variation and deliberate disruption of the pattern.

'Write it in fire across the night: / Some men are more or less all right.' Thus Wendy Cope's fireworks couplet for the Salisbury Literary Festival. The first line begins with an inverted first foot but is thereafter regularly iambic: 'in fire across the night'; three iambs. The second line is bathetic rhythmically but actually also regular – an iambic tetrameter. The humour comes from the scarcely differentiated sounds of 'are', 'more' and 'or', while the line's rhythmic template nevertheless demands that 'more' takes the stress.

What is true of metre is true of the line. The Platonic line is a unit of sense and cadence – which poets are entitled to disrupt, *enjoined* to disrupt – as long as they know what they are disrupting and why they are disrupting it. You can't just guess.

# Chapter Five

## Lyric

In *The Bostonians*, Henry James says the frigid, Sapphic Olive Chancellor was 'a spinster as Shelley was a lyric poet, as the month of August is sultry'. James takes it for granted we know what a lyric poet is. As identifiable as the hot month of August. We take it for granted, too. But what does it actually mean?

This is Seamus Heaney, in 'The Government of the Tongue', talking about the end of Elizabeth Bishop's poem 'At the Fishhouses': '[the lines] possess that *sine qua non* of all lyric utterance, a completely persuasive inner cadence which is deeply intimate with the laden water of the full tide.' I think he means that the sound of the lines somehow conjures the presence of the water they describe. A sort of mimesis that *all* lyric poetry allegedly possesses. Your guess is as good as mine.

If we look at the introduction to R. T. Davies's *Medieval English Lyrics*, we discover the lyric manifests singular variety. 'These lyrics are conspicuously varied: their range frequently surprises. But they were written by a diversity of people in the course of four centuries, by learned men in serious and in trivial mood, and by women running comfortable households in the country, by court entertainers and by civil servants, by noblemen and by saints...' It isn't obvious what 'lyric' entails. The word has a wide penumbra. It seems to be the fall-back category, the catch-all, when other more obvious categories are

inapplicable: epic poetry, narrative poetry. Like many categories, its catchment area, too, has shifted over time – like, say, the
elegy, which in Latin was originally a verse form of alternating
hexameters and pentameters, with no restriction of subject.
Hence Donne's (sexually explicit) elegy 'On His Mistris Going
to Bed'. It also included the lament for a person's death – the
connotation it now carries.

The word 'lyric' comes from the Greek word for 'lyre' and
it originally meant words that were accompanied by music.
Sappho, Quiller-Couch tells us, 'plucked her passion from the
lyre'. But he is quick to point out that, except for Burns, Tom
Moore, Heinrich Heine and Béranger, you will find very little
nineteenth-century poetry written 'primarily *to be sung*'. This
meaning still survives in the song lyrics of, say, Radiohead or
Coldplay. In poetry, the musical accompaniment – there impli-
citly in Wyatt's 'My lute awake!, performe the laste' and 'Blame
not my lute!' – gradually atrophied and the words stood alone.
But the idea of song is still important. It implies brevity and
simplicity. Songs are not noted for their complexity. The lyric is
a spontaneous overflow of powerful feeling – in Wordsworth's
famous phrase – an emotional outburst, primarily appropri-
ate to the first person singular, though possible perhaps in a
dramatic monologue. Hence Flaubert's association of lyricism
with sexual excitement and the prospect of ejaculation – verbal
and sexual. This is a letter to Louise Colet (15 July 1853): 'Life!
Life! To have erections! That is everything, the only thing that
counts! That is why I so love lyricism. It seems to me the most
natural form of poetry – poetry in all its nakedness and freedom.'

T. S. Eliot in *The Use of Poetry and the Use of Criticism* quotes
T. E. Hulme with approval – and this approval is in reality an
attack on Wordsworth's definition of poetry as 'the spontan-

eous overflow of powerful feeling'. I've quoted it already in this
book. Here it is again, for a different purpose:

> There is a general tendency to think that verse means little
> else than the expression of unsatisfied emotion... The
> great aim is accurate, precise and definite description. The
> first thing is to realise how extraordinarily difficult this is...
> Language has its own special nature, its own conventions
> and communal ideas. It is only by a concentrated effort of
> mind that you can hold it fixed to your own purpose.

This Hulme passage perhaps explains why, in the twentieth century, we are no longer certain, as Henry James was, what a lyric
poet might be. Eliot can be very musical, ravishingly musical,
but no one would describe him as a lyric poet. (In his essay
on Yeats in *On Poetry and Poets*, 1957, Eliot counter-distinguishes
himself from Yeats: 'I have spoken of him as having been a
lyric poet – in a sense in which I should not think of myself, for
instance, as lyric.')

Though he quotes Hulme, Eliot, of course, was capable *in
propria persona* of letting the afflatus out of the idea of poetry
as self-expression. Here he is on Dr Johnson's poetry (in *On
Poetry and Poets*): 'Those who demand of poetry a daydream, or
a metamorphosis of their own feeble desires and lusts, or what
they believe to be "intensity" of passion, will not find much
in Johnson. He is like Pope and Dryden, Crabbe and Landor,
a poet for those who want poetry and not something else,
some stay for their own vanity...' The perspective is that of the
reader, rather than the practitioner (as it is the practitioner in
Hulme), but the fundamental idea is the same. Poetry isn't the
unbridled expression of emotion.

Or allegedly 'powerful feeling'. I am reminded of Christopher Tietjens upbraiding Vincent MacMaster at the beginning of *Parade's End*. MacMaster is the editor of Dante Gabriel Rossetti – whom Tietjens denounces as 'loathsome' for justifying libido by invoking Love and inflecting adultery with spirituality – in essence, sentimentalising lust, what Eliot called the 'metamorphosis of their own feeble desires'. Dante, by contrast, packs off Paolo and Francesca 'very properly to Hell' – 'and no bones about it', adds Tietjens. Only in a world where feeling is exclusively prized are morality and complication suspended.

In the twentieth century, accuracy and precision arrive. Irony about strong emotion arrives. And the lyric becomes slightly suspect. In Seamus Heaney's *The Government of the Tongue*, we find the idea of pure lyric utterance questioned in the introductory essay, 'The Interesting Case of Nero, Chekhov's Cognac and a Knocker'. Nero's irresponsibility – fiddling while Rome burned – becomes a figure for the ethical complication attendant on pure art. Wilfred Owen is a key figure in Heaney's argument: Owen in his exemplary way attacks the lyric impulse to beautification, ironically citing the Horatian assertion that it is beautiful to die for one's country. But then Heaney remembers teaching Owen's poetry and his inconvenient impulse to criticise Owen's many artistic awkwardnesses. Over-writing is Heaney's central charge. It's a complicated essay whose hero is Chekhov, paying his ethical dues by a dutiful trip to Sakhalin's convict colony, then afterwards indulging his artistic bent – an indulgence figured in Heaney's essay by the brandy Chekhov drank on arrival in Sakhalin until he was drunk. Drunk and irresponsible. Heaney can see, all too clearly, that the ethical impulse can easily betray the poet into the prescriptive, into propaganda.

Beautification – tarting things up – has always been associated with the lyric. That and exaggerated feeling. In Chapter 7 of *Dead Souls*, Gogol makes a distinction between the Gogolian writer and the writer who offers his reader 'the smoke of illusion... obscuring the sadness of life and showing them man as a thing of beauty'. (Of course, it is possible to exaggerate the sadness of life and achieve a similar afflatus.) This kind of writer is contrasted with the Gogolian writer 'who has ventured to bring into the open what is ever before one's eyes' – that is, the dreary, the ridiculous and the trifling. But the first kind of writer is favoured by readers: 'contemporary judgment does not allow the high laughter of delight a worthy place side by side with lofty *lyrical* emotion' [my italics]. Gogol died in 1852: he is the father of Chekhov's banal familiarity, his provincial observations, his characters' yearning for exaltation and excitement. Gogol gives a whole page over to what people say when they are playing cards.

In Part 5, Chapter 10 of *The Unbearable Lightness of Being*, Kundera distinguishes between two types of womaniser: one who is searching for the ideal woman, and one who wishes to experience the variety of women. The first type Kundera designates as lyrical: 'The obsession of the former is *lyrical*: what they seek in women is themselves, their ideal, and since an ideal is by definition something that can never be found, they are disappointed again and again.' The ideal – an important part of the word 'lyric'.

The lyric depends for its effect and its authenticity on its evident sincerity – it is an effusion, a single emotion. Are there any lyrics which are complicated? Come live with me and be my love. All those carpe diems. My luv is like a red red rose. Doesn't the lyric offer – if not a downright noble lie – at the very least a simplification? Hermann Hesse's lyrics for Richard Strauss's 'Four Last Songs' say that you die, but you live eternally. You see? That's why we say: he *burst* into song. And good poets are tempted, too. As I said earlier, Seamus Heaney's *Seeing Things* is balanced, like its title, between the visionary and the delusional. It entertains poetic fictions, knowingly, and indulges, all the time aware, impossible possibilities.

'Sumer is icumen in' is the *song* of the cuckoo. It expresses one thing: eternal summer, repetitive, ceaseless summer, like the ceaseless song of the cuckoo. It never mentions winter.

Sometimes we think we need this kind of poetry. In prose fiction, the movement over three centuries has been away from the impossible, the exaggerated, and towards the plausible. From the picaresque of *Tom Jones* to the pattens and muddy lanes of Jane Austen sixty years later. Once realism is established, of course, there is a counter-impulse to magic realism, to the exciting if implausible. The history of literature is the history of restlessness, of discontent, of boredom, of an appetite for aesthetic excitement.

Zbigniew Herbert's 'Arion' ('the Grecian Caruso') is a poem about the lyric voice – the lyric voice meaning the expression of the idyllic, the poetic fiction of Arcadia. Herbert ironises it – as you might expect. When Arion sings, we're told that

> The crowns blacken on the tyrants' heads
> and the sellers of onion cakes
> for the first time err in their figures to their own disadvantage

Ho yus, as William Brown would say.

But in 'Three Studies on the Subject of Realism', it is obvious that Herbert isn't keen on its opposite either. There, he sees realism as, first, a corrective flight from a collective sentimental delusion that life is a pretty pastoral idyll. Then he considers a version of the Dutch school of painting – severe, uncensored reality ('everything in heavy and dull brown ochre') where life is an extended, unmitigated unhappiness of mean streets and mean hearts, demanding political change, revolutionary change: 'the clear water of fresh floods / is requested by the brush'. The consequence, in Part 3, is the destruction of art because it is evaluated on political grounds. It is destroyed by simplification:

> ...divided into the right side and the left side
> who know only two colours
> colour yes and colour no...

Subtlety, the use of pastels, the 'perhaps' in the palette, is postponed and promised for later. In this account, it is easy to see that communist realism is as simplifying as the lyricism of Arion: 'the inventors of simple symbols / open palms and clenched fists.' The fellow-travelling doves of Picasso, as it were.

So, in Herbert's 'Three Studies on the Subject of Realism', two routes to the same end – the lyric dream. The lyric as temptation, the air-brushed, unblemished apple. Super-sweet. As Kundera also knows in *Life is Elsewhere*: 'revolutions are lyrical and in need of lyricism.'

Milan Kundera's *Life is Elsewhere* analyses the connection between the lyric impulse and fatal political simplification. His hero, however, is not a bad poet (see *Testaments Betrayed*, page 233, for Kundera's explicit endorsement of his talent). Kundera is subtle enough, intelligent enough, to know that Jaromil represents a permanent human impulse, the aspiration to beauty, to perfection – which, however, is always at the mercy of the pratfall, the splayed, obscene banana skin, insomniac irony. The lyric speaks to a permanent, genuine human need. But a need does not logically require satisfaction. 'It is a truth universally acknowledged, that a single man in possession of a good fortune, must be in want of a wife.' Demand, though, does not guarantee supply. If Jane Austen answers the want postulated in her famous opening sentence, it proves to be a complicated answer.

Kundera is useful in placing the lyric for us. Its scope has narrowed from those medieval lyrics. Its desire for perfection has undergone purification. It is genuine but it is saccharine – because it does not answer to reality, rather to the emotional theorem. For example, ideally, we would all like to be truthful. But think of Gregers Werle, the catastrophic truth-teller in Ibsen's *The Wild Duck*... 'Lyrical souls who like to preach the abolition of secrets and the transparency of private life do not realise the nature of the process they are unleashing. The starting point of totalitarianism resembles the beginning of *The Trial*: you'll be taken unawares in your bed.' (Kundera: *The Art of the Novel*.) But this doesn't go far enough. Let me tease out its implications. The lyric addresses our yearning for an ideal – but the high-minded desire to discover a theorem soon declines into our desire to lay down the law. Ian McEwan went to a political conference sometime in the late 1970s where the correct Leftist attitude to sex was discussed. In bed, we are naked, incorrect, indecent and improper, as well as unguarded. Once disclose this site of impropriety and two consequences follow. First, a law is passed – a private member's bill perhaps, but widely supported by both sides of the hypocritical House – stipulating that clothes should be worn in bed. Second, and worse, the excitement of indecency evaporates. We become like the man on the building site barely looking at the bare breasts on page three of his tabloid before he turns the page. We need excitement.

'The lyric is the expression of a self-revealing subjectivity,' writes Kundera in *The Art of the Novel*. The danger of the lyric impulse is that it over-prizes subjectivity, over-prizes the *expression* of emotion. We're back to Wordsworth's 'spontaneous overflow of powerful feeling'. But it isn't simply the overflow. It is that the emotion is thought to be irresistible, privileged, brushing all obstacles aside – as George Eliot ruefully noted. In *Middlemarch*, Chapter XXXI, she writes: 'There are many wonderful mixtures in the world which are all alike called love, and claim the privileges of a sublime rage which is an apology for everything (in literature and the drama).' This is why a literary classicist like T. S. Eliot in *After Strange Gods* will attack the self-justifying centrality of strong feeling in the romantic imagination.

Has anyone, in recent times, advocated the centrality of strong feeling in poetry? Ian Hamilton, deliberately reacting against T. S. Eliot, envisaged a poetry with feeling as its engine, as its heart. 'I think I feel that if you are a lyric poet of the "miraculous" persuasion, then you will never properly "grow up".' What exactly did Hamilton mean by 'miraculous'? Partly that the poems came unbidden, out of experience: the poet didn't go looking for subjects. Partly that poetry of this kind could perform miracles. This is from a conversation with Peter Dale in *Agenda* (summer 1993): 'one knew that in life ordinary speech made little difference, couldn't save the other person from death or from illness. Poetic speech might work differently... While writing a poem, one could have the illusion that one was talking in a magic way to the subject of the poem. One might even think that this is doing some good, making things better.'

The one saving word here is 'illusion'. In his preface to *Fifty Poems* (1988), Hamilton wrote: 'But did I truly think that poetry, if perfect, could bring back the dead? In some way, yes, I think I did.' So, an illusion embraced by the young Hamilton – and not exactly disowned by the older Hamilton. Certainly not mocked, as it might be by, say, the Beckett of *Krapp's Last Tape*. Exhibited, rather, as impossible but admirable and idealistic.

The idea of poetic truth – that beauty is truth, truth beauty – is hard to expunge, sentimental though it is. Auden, in his essay on Robert Frost, points out that this motto is spoken by the urn, not Keats, and that it sums up a kind of poetry where the unpleasant and awkward is excluded. I don't think Auden is quite right. In the ode, 'evils and problems' are present but subtly veiled. Keats, who formulated the fiction, knows it to be a fiction, as he demonstrates within the poem. Is it possible that Keats *meant* something by this impacted gnomic chiasmus? I think it is. The poem quite consciously offers readers a contradiction between the classical stillness of the urn and the scenes depicted on its panels. But Keats's level tone, his muted tone, matches the quietness of the urn, its 'cold pastoral'. The first line tells us much: first, that the urn is intact, unbroken; second, that it is an '*unravished* bride'. Why *this* metaphor? Initially, we think Keats is balancing mortality and eternity. The lovers on the vase will last, unlike real flesh and blood, yet they will never achieve consummation. 'She cannot fade, though thou hast not thy bliss, / Forever wilt thou love, and she be fair!' The consolation of art is youth on perpetual pause – the transcendence of the human and the physical. And this element is undoubtedly there in Keats's poem but it does not engage with the motto: 'Beauty is truth, truth beauty.'

The link is the scene with its *beauty* – 'happy, happy love' – and the *truth* of what is actually depicted – a rape scene: 'What maidens *loth*'; 'What *struggle* to escape'; 'maidens *overwrought*'. Three telling words only, but they are enough. And they are enough even if one of them – 'overwrought' – also refers to the decoration on the urn.

Keats manages something hypnotic by his tone. In *Death in the Afternoon*, Hemingway comments on a photograph of a picador pic-ing a bull. He points out that the bull's head is under the horse's body, that the horse's front feet are off the ground because the bull's horn is in its belly. Then Hemingway invites us to consider the horse's calm head – an effect achieved, he says, by the confident knees of the picador. In his 'Ode on a Grecian Urn', Keats brings off a similar feat. We are persuaded that nothing untoward is afoot, despite that 'trodden weed'.

The sacrifice of the heifer involves a similar double-take. As presented, the 'little town' is silent, deserted, 'peaceful', 'pious'. As Keats speculates about the alternative locations – riverside, sea shore, mountainside – we forget the blood-letting to come, distracted by Keats's bedside manner, his marble calm. Another truth beautified by the imagination. The 'Ode on a Grecian Urn' is the perfect illustration of Keatsian 'negative capability', suspended between truth and beauty, two Siamese twins. And the perfect illustration of the lyric and what it means in relation to reality.

# Chapter Six

## *Metaphor*

It is sometimes said that, as a poetic procedure, metaphor is more profound than simile. The late William Scammell took this view. And he took it from T. S. Eliot. I'm not sure there is any justification for thinking this true. After all, the metaphor and the simile are fundamentally the same mechanism – a comparison between two things which insists on a likeness in spite of obvious differences. For example: imagine a balding man with a comb-over who is trapped in a high wind. Metaphor: the comet of his hair streamed in the wind. Simile: his hair streamed from the side of his head like a comet. The simile's form, the use of 'like', makes the comparison more straightforward. I think William Scammell mistrusted straightforwardness.

This is Eliot in his 1929 essay on Dante, comparing Dante and Shakespeare. Eliot takes the famous comparison of the benighted crowd of sinners looking at Virgil and Dante like an old tailor squinting at the eye of his needle ('come vecchio sartor fa nella cruna') and sets beside it three lines from *Antony and Cleopatra*, describing the dead Cleopatra:

> she looks like sleep,
> As she would catch another Antony
> In her strong toil of grace.

The dead Cleopatra doesn't look dead. She seems asleep. She looks capable of exerting the power of her undiminished beauty on men even in death.

The linguistic puzzle here is in the apparent paradox of effort ('strong toil') applied to a state usually thought to be the opposite of effortful. Grace isn't achieved by effort or art. It is bestowed. However, this isn't Shakespeare's intended meaning. By 'toil', Shakespeare means 'net'.

Does Eliot know this?

> The image of Shakespeare's is much more complicated than Dante's, and more complicated than it looks. It has the grammatical form of a kind of simile (the 'as if' form) but of course 'catch in her toil' is a metaphor. But whereas the simile of Dante is *merely* [my italics] to make you see more clearly how the people looked, and is explanatory, the figure of Shakespeare is expansive rather than intensive; its purpose is to *add* to what you see… a reminder of that fascination of Cleopatra which shaped her history and that of the world, and of that fascination being so strong that it prevails even in death.

Eliot isn't clear here – not until the final phrase. He's amplifying, rather emptily. In fact, he concludes that Shakespeare's language 'is more elusive [than Dante's]' and his ideas 'less possible to convey without close knowledge of the English language'. None of this would be necessary if Eliot told us what 'toil' means. But you need a close knowledge of the English language to do that. Shakespeare, in this example, is only less translatable than Dante if you don't know exactly what he means, but are merely dealing with his drift.

However, he does voice the idea that metaphor is richer,

more expansive, than simile. His exegesis, though, may be responsible for the putative expansiveness – rather than the metaphor itself. Which says that Cleopatra's beauty is a strong net.

The other common criticism of the simile is that it tends to the purely visual. Henry James, though barely distinguishing between metaphor and simile, writes, in a review of Flaubert's Correspondence (1893): 'No one will care for him at all who does not care for his metaphors, and those moreover who care most for these will be discreet enough to admit that even a style rich in similes is limited when it renders only the visible. The invisible Flaubert scarcely touches...'

Of course, the simile isn't limited to the visible. Sylvia Plath's 'Wuthering Heights': 'the wind / Pours by like destiny.'

But why is the simile thought inferior? I repeat, metaphor and simile share a mechanism: one thing is compared to another thing in a way that overrides apparent differences. More, the apparent, flagrant differences are essential to the operation of a good metaphor or simile.

All simile involves calculation, mental arithmetic that human beings perform naturally at phenomenal speeds. In any simile, we eliminate the points of dissimilarity to arrive promptly at the point of just similarity – for example, between decaying magnolia petals and used toilet paper. The differences are plentiful, the similarity, the coincidence singular. I call this the calculus of metaphor. It is a calculation all human beings perform intuitively, speedily.

*However*: it is a mental operation possible only if you know both halves of the equation. If $x = y$, you need to know the value of $x$ and the value of $y$. Stendhal in *Histoire de la peinture en Italie*: 'you can't convey the reality of anything – including emotion – if the reader hasn't experienced the thing himself.

No amount of description will do it.'

We can test that with the magnolia's fallen petals like used toilet paper. We know, all of us, what used toilet paper looks like. The effectiveness of the metaphor is cognate with the gap between petals and toilet paper.

Aristotle says in the *Poetics* that metaphor is 'a sign of genius, since a good metaphor implies an intuitive perception of the *similarity in dissimilarity*'. *Discordia concors*. Agreement in disagreement. In disagreement, agreement. For a metaphor or simile to work, there must be an obvious distance between the tenor and vehicle, between the petal and the smutched toilet paper. There should be a slight shock. The effective simile is also a self-conscious simile – in a word, art.

If you compared crumpled snow to frost – or even to a white blanket – there would be no shock, no gap for the spark of similitude to cross. How dead, how stale, is a blanket of snow. We no longer even register the blanket as a blanket.

However... the epic simile is a special case of the calculus where, as it were, the sum, the arithmetic, is deliberately longer. In Matthew Arnold's *Sohrab and Rustum*, the Griffin seal on Sohrab's arm shows he is the son of Rustum. Arnold compares, at length, over ten lines, the Griffin seal to the workmanship of a Chinese potter:

> and near the shoulder bared his arm,
> And show'd a sign in faint vermilion points
> Prick'd; as a cunning workman, in Pekin,
> Pricks with vermilion some clear porcelain vase,
> An emperor's gift – at early morn he paints,
> And all day long, and, when night comes, the lamp
> Lights up his studious forehead and thin hands –

So delicately prick'd the sign appear'd
On Sohrab's arm, the sign of Rustum's seal.

Unquestionably, this beautiful simile works. But how does it work?

The epic simile differs from the simple simile because, initially, there is no discordia, the comparison is obvious: the faint vermilion points pricked on Sohrab's arm are like, exactly like, 'pricks with vermilion' on some porcelain vase. The epic simile then proceeds to accumulate difference: the lamp, the studious forehead, those *thin* hands. These are details which have no bearing on the point of comparison – details which take us away from the comparison. The *implicit* divergencies of the simple simile are spelled out in the epic simile – before the comparison is again insisted on.

Traditionally, the conceit, the metaphysical conceit, is a comparison in which the *appropriateness* and justice of the comparison have to be spelled out and argued – because initially the comparison seems so unlikely. For example, in Donne's 'A Valediction: forbidding mourning', we encounter the notorious 'stiffe twin compasses'.

If they [our soules] be two, they are two so
As stiffe twin compasses are two,
Thy soule the fixt foot, makes no show
To move, but doth, if th'other doe.

And though it in the centre sit,
Yet when the other far doth roam,
It leanes, and hearkens after it,
And growes erect, as that comes home.

> Such wilt thou be to mee, who must
> Like th'other foot, obliquely runne;
> Thy firmnes makes my circle just,
> And makes me end, where I begunne.

Dr Johnson was impatient with the conceit. In his essay on Abraham Cowley, he describes the conceit as a far-fetched comparison that 'is not worth the carriage'. You might think, from Johnson's irritation, that the conceit was commonplace in metaphysical poetry. In fact, there aren't many examples in Donne. It is a comparative rarity. His exasperation, too, can be accounted for by his analysis of the conceit's operations. Helen Gardner, following Johnson, accepts that the conceit comes with its own justification – like a lawyer establishing an alibi, instance by instance, point by point. But this is to misplace the emphasis. The conceit isn't a dogged justification. It is an ebullient amplification. It rejoices in its own ingenuity. It isn't in the least defensive. It is exfoliation for its own sake. Take 'The Flea': how is the loss of virginity like a flea bite? Like this and like this and like this. The conceit is the opposite of the epic simile which maximises the distance between the two things being compared – to maximise the satisfaction of closure when it eventually comes like a deferred orgasm. The conceit is inventive, witty – a multiple orgasm.

The attachment between the two lovers, their fundamental inseparability, is expounded at some length. No, not 'expounded' – rather, *elaborated*. The key adjective, though, is 'stiffe' – not, as some commentators have thought, a sexual reference, but an index of the reluctance with which the lovers are parted.

Longinus believed metaphor to be at the heart of poetry. Likewise Aristotle: 'the greatest thing by far is to be a master of metaphor.' Dryden (attacking Shakespeare's dense verbal texture) differed: ''Tis not that I would explode the use of metaphors from passions, for Longinus thinks 'em necessary to raise it: but to use 'em at every word, to say nothing without a metaphor, a simile, an image, or description, is, I doubt, to smell a little too strongly of the buskin.'

Again, it is instructive to go to prose writers to see what our undisclosed assumptions about metaphor are. Pauline Melville, an English novelist of Guyanese extraction, has written about her attempt with a Guyanese cousin to compile a Wapichan dictionary. Wapichan is a major Guyanese dialect: 'There is poetry in the language, too. The word for cobweb – *soo-shimeak* – translates as "spider's hammock" and *kadakob*, the word for "big-mouthed catfish", is sometimes used for "politician". The same sort of poetry is embedded in English, of course, but with centuries of usage it's easy to forget that the word "daisy" originally meant "day's eye".' The daisy is like a sun, therefore, or like a child's drawing of the sun. In my notebook, I have daisies 'like fried eggs'.

In 'Black Sheep: 1937', a section about Osip Mandelstam in my epic poem *History: the Home-Movie*, Mandelstam goes back to his flat in Moscow after exile in Voronezh: 'Spiders sprawl in their hammocks.' I have my own *soo-shimeak* because metaphor is a faculty common to all human beings. So I find it odd that some critics find metaphor too studied to be natural – Dryden, for one.

Pauline Melville agrees with Aristotle. If there is inadvertent poetry in the language, it is because language is naturally metaphorical. The anonymous person who thought of skinhead had a metaphorical gift – as had the Australian who came up with 'laying a cable' for taking a shit, or 'talking to the big white telephone' for throwing up, or 'technicolour yawn' for vomit.

It is possible that these coinages may be the genius of Barry Humphries, who, with the illustrator Nick Garland, featured both sayings in their *Private Eye* strip cartoon, *Barry McKenzie*. The point is still valid. I remember my five-year-old daughter describing a juggler as a man sharing balls between his hands. It was inadvertent poetry when she said it and authenticated when I stole it for inclusion in one of my poems.

Juggling takes me straight to Jorge Luis Borges. Borges, in his *Paris Review* interview, argues against metaphor for two reasons. First, everyone comes up with the same metaphors. Second, original metaphors are contrived and artificial: even as they strive to be original, they achieve only shallow verbal effects:

> When I was a young man I was always hunting for new metaphors. Then I found that really good metaphors are always the same. I mean, you compare time to a road, death to sleeping, life to dreaming, and those are the great metaphors in literature because they correspond to something essential. If you invent metaphors, they are apt to be surprising during the fraction of a second, but they strike no deep emotion whatever. If you think of life as a dream, that is a thought, a thought that is real, or at least that most men are bound to have, no? 'What oft was thought but ne'er so well expressed.' I think that's better than the idea of shocking people, than finding connections between things that have never been connected before, because there is no real connection, so the whole thing is a kind of juggling.

I think there is a way of reconciling and answering these two strands of Borges's argument. An original metaphor is always read with an act of recognition. We are surprised but recognise the justice of the comparison. The sensation of recognition always accompanies the shock, the surprise, of discovery, because metaphor is impossible if both terms are not previously known. What is new is the relationship, the kinship – which was, it seems, always there, waiting to be found. When Marianne Moore compares the flight of a butterfly to the sight of wreckage out at sea – we see the justice and we confirm the occult relationship between the two separate things.

Essentially, these objections to metaphor – a completely natural resource – reflect a mistrust of art, a sentimental yearning for artlessness. But all art involves choice. It involves a conscious process.

Borges fails to understand the purpose of metaphor – which is one of heightened clarification. To appreciate the justice of the implied comparison, we have to scrutinise both halves of the equation. Marianne Moore compares a lion's head to a chrysanthemum. We visualise both before we underwrite the comparison: all metaphor, all simile makes us look again, think again, re-think. Borges's confusion here is between a shared ability, facility, function – which we all have quite naturally – and the results of that function. He prefers the obvious to the unusual. (I will say more about the crucial requirement of swiftness in metaphor later.)

In fact, even the most apparently original metaphors are sometimes shared – not only the time-is-a-road kind. For example, I described Negro chest hair as peppercorns of hair in 'A Journey to Greece', an image I later discovered in Saul Bellow's *Henderson the Rain King*: 'His hair grew tight and small, peppercorn style, in tiny droplike curls.' In my copy of Golding's *Darkness Visible*, I have a pencilled exclamation mark in the margin beside 'All his hair was gone on that side, and on the other, shrivelled to peppercorn dots.' Chronologically, Bellow is first, I am second, and Golding is a close third. In reality, we are simultaneous, writers struck by the same idea – which confirms my argument that all metaphor involves recognition.

Or there is that notorious, contrived yet strangely promiscuous image of a woman's behind like an inverted satin heart on a Valentine's card – shared four ways by Updike, Nabokov, Bellow and Martin Amis. Bellow (*Humboldt's Gift*): 'You have a bottom like a white valentine greeting.' Nabokov (*Bend Sinister*): 'her rump, which in those days of tight skirts, looked like an inverted heart.' Updike (*Rabbit Redux*): 'the upside-down valentine of a woman's satin rear.' Amis (*The Pregnant Widow*) is describing Gloria Beautyman's behind: 'Later that same day, playing solitaire, Keith made an exact visual match: the ace of hearts. In two dimensions, then. And hearts: hearts. Which wasn't the right suit.' Why this four-way coincidence? I think men look hard at women's arses. That's all.

Or I thought so until I read May-Lan Tan's short story 'New Jersey' (2014) in which one girl says of another girl's behind, 'It looks good that way. Like an upside-down heart.' From which I conclude that women also look at women's behinds. So: a *five-way* coincidence.

But by and large there will be difference, not coincidence.

We are all familiar with Archibald MacLeish's obiter dictum that poetry should not mean, but be. (A convenient excuse never to explain the meaning of any poem.) We also know that William Carlos Williams adjured us: no ideas but in things. We think we know what this means. We think it means that abstractions are a curse and that poetry's currency is the concrete. A rather different proposition from MacLeish's but sometimes the two are conflated.

Actually, that's not what Williams meant at all. The apophthegm comes from his poem 'A Sort of a Song': the argument

of this poem is that metaphor is the only way we have of establishing real contact between the human mind and the reality
outside us. Metaphor is a way of healing the mind–body dual-
ism. This is a rather more sophisticated proposition than the
anti-intellectual sounding 'no ideas but in things'.

> Let the snake wait under
> his weed
> and the writing
> be of words, slow and quick, sharp
> to strike, quiet to wait,
> sleepless.
> – through metaphor to reconcile
> the people and the stones.
> Compose. (No ideas
> but in things) Invent!
> Saxifrage is my flower that splits
> the rocks.

We have the snake and we have the words. We make the
words approximate to the snake: they, too, strike and wait. The
flower, saxifrage, does the apparently impossible: it splits rocks.
Its name is crucial to the poem's point. It represents an ideal
of poetic language – in which the thing being described and
the language describing it are completely identical. The thing,
the rock-splitting flower, and its name, the word 'saxifrage',
are identical. Saxifrage, a perennial herb, is Latin for 'breaking
rocks'. The word is an exact fit to reality. (You could also say,
sceptically, that it was functionally tautological, and begged
the question.) The gap between the signifier and the signified,
between mind and reality, is non-existent.

So what do the last two lines mean? 'Saxifrage is my flower

that splits / the rocks.' The problem set by Williams is to make words correspond to reality – as exactly as the word 'saxifrage' does. That word figuratively splits the rock: the name itself is a metaphor.

Let me return to the idea that metaphor is 'expansion' – metaphor as vagueness. There is an uncollected Ted Hughes poem, 'The Pike', about a pike in a reservoir. It begins: 'In the reservoir, behind the mirror // The pike...' It is a brilliant opening: we quickly translate 'the mirror' to the reflected light on the surface of the water, but not before there has lodged the sinister, surreal, impossible idea of a pike behind a mirror, haunting the ordinary, the everyday. We eliminate the idea but its taste remains in our mouth. Human beings like clarification. They also like mystery, a kind of intoxicated Keatsian negative capability. Debussy said Turner was the 'finest creator of mystery in the history of art'. (Quoted by Stephen Plaistow: Radio 3 *CD Review* 'Building a Library': Debussy's Preludes Book II.) The appeal of vagueness afflicts even poets. Auden, in *The Table Talk of W. H. Auden* by Alan Ansen, said on 30 October 1947: 'I'm doing a selected edition of Pope. Some of the lines are wonderful – "Bare the mean Heart that lurks beneath a Star." You know it's the Garter, and yet somehow it isn't...' In other words, the simple *sense* of the line is augmented by *non-sense* – and that semantic penumbra appeals to Auden. To some amateurs, of course, the point of poetry is its failure to mean anything specific. But you don't expect poets and 'experts' to welcome an art of accidentals and mumbo-jumbo.

You would be wrong. I just mentioned Keats. Sean O'Brien invoked him too (*Guardian* Review, 8 March 2008) while introducing the Faber series 'Great Poets of the Twentieth Century':

To do so [read poetry] requires us to claim that imaginative space, and to live with Keats's 'uncertainties, Mysteries,
doubts', rather than rush to conclude and summarise. Part
of what Eliot called 'the shock of poetry' lies in the fact that
what it offers is often both instinctively recognisable and at
the same time resistant to interpretation – a three-dimen-
sional experience for the imagination, *not a mere scanning of
captions*... [my italics]

In the same series, Nicholas Wroe advised readers not to worry
about meaning (*Guardian*, 11 March 2008):

perhaps the other piece of advice is, counter-intuitively,
don't get too hung up on meaning. If these poets had
wanted to give a straightforward instruction or a puzzle
with an answer they wouldn't have done it in poetry. So
trust them. They are indisputably geniuses and you are
entirely secure in their hands. Allow the words and rhythms
to wash over you.

Compare Erica Wagner in *The Times* (12 November 2005)
'reviewing' the last book of Michael Donaghy:

Please: don't be put off. On the inside-jacket flap of Michael
Donaghy's final collection of poems, his work is described
as 'metaphysically dense'. Yes, 'emotionally direct' and
'perfectly crafted' too, but the reference to metaphysics
you may find alarming. I did. Just look at the beautiful
photograph of Donaghy's son, Ruari, that gives this slim
volume with its reassuring title an immediate appeal. Now
open the book and allow Donaghy's work to flow around
you like water.

Perhaps all these statements go back to Helen Gardner's *The Art of T. S. Eliot*: 'It is better, in reading poetry of this kind, to trouble too little about the "meaning" than to trouble too much. If there are passages whose meaning seems elusive, where we feel we are "missing the point", we should read on, preferably aloud... We must find the meaning in the reading...'

I believe that the first and most important question you can ask a poem is 'what does it mean?' The poet, unless he is John Ashbery, relies on his reader to try to make sense of the poem, to make sense of each line, each word. When Eliot writes in 'Prufrock' that the evening is laid out against the sky 'like a patient etherized upon a table', he doesn't expect Terry Eagleton's 'explanation' that the baffling simile is a defining aspect of modernism. He expects his reader to think in what way the comparison is justified – to see that he, Eliot, is refining a standard poetic trope of the sunset as blood. We will get nowhere with poetry if we stall at the start and decide it cannot be understood. Even Auden knows the real meaning of 'the mean Heart that lies beneath a Star' – the decoration of the Order of the Garter. Unless we know what a poem means, we cannot judge the success or failure of its local effects.

Sean O'Brien is the most sophisticated advocate of poetry as oracle rather than Christmas cracker. He forges an alliance with Eliot and Keats. Neither is a true ally. Of course, it is true that poetry in the twentieth century became more difficult – but poetry has always been difficult, even the simple poetry of *Lyrical Ballads*. The poems in *Lyrical Ballads* invoke the ballad and yet deny the ballad's defining characteristic – a poem like 'Simon Lee' denies story, refuses narrative. *Lyrical Ballads* exists in aesthetic contradiction – so simple, so transparent, it is opaque. The Browning Society was founded to explain Browning's difficult poetry – which no longer seems difficult. This is partly because, by now, readers do not expect to understand poetry. In *The Use of Poetry*, Eliot said that everyone has heard of stage fright. No one, though, he says, talks about gallery fright – the paralysing fear of not understanding.

Here is Keats's definition of negative capability: 'that is, when a man is capable of being in uncertainties, Mysteries, doubts, without any irritable reaching after fact and reason.' But this isn't so vague when applied to 'Ode on a Grecian Urn'. It is about the ability of the imagination to encompass opposites – as I have already argued.

To recapitulate: 'Thou still unravished bride of quietness' has a rape scene depicted on one of its panels – 'What maidens loth?' – i.e. unwilling. 'What struggle to escape?' Yet the ode manages to beautify this scene:

> Bold Lover, never, never canst thou kiss,
> Though winning near the goal – yet, do not grieve;
> She cannot fade, though thou hast not thy bliss,
> For ever wilt thou love, and she be fair!

The rapist is there only in the significantly muted adjective 'bold' in 'Bold Lover'. And the libido has been given a makeover: 'For ever wilt thou love…' *Love?* In the other odes, Keats is interested in the moments of opposition, of liminality: when autumn's ripeness tilts into decay; when joy's grape is burst and 'His Soul shall taste the sadness of her might [melancholy's might].'

Underneath this is Keats's conviction that the imagination can envision and realise the impossible – like Adam's dream, from which he awoke to find it truth. 'Ode to Psyche' is another good example: Psyche is a dead deity ('O latest born and loveliest vision far / Of all Olympus' *faded* hierarchy…') but by the end of the poem, Keats has built a temple (a 'fane') 'in some untrodden region of my mind' – and Psyche's beloved Cupid is about to enter by the open *casement*. And Cupid is *warm*... The dead has been brought to life, though not in the way envisioned by Ian Hamilton.

How does this affect O'Brien? It argues against him by saying that the contradictions can be explained, that they are rational rather than enigmatic and insoluble.

And Eliot? O'Brien has manufactured his quotation about the 'shock' of poetry. Eliot in 'Dante' says: 'The experience of a poem is the experience both of a moment and of a lifetime. It is very much like our intenser experiences of other human beings. There is a first, or an early moment which is unique, of shock and surprise [this is where O'Brien is coming from], even terror, which, though never forgotten completely, is bedded down in a deeper and calmer feeling.' Eliot is talking about love at first sight, the *coup de foudre* – and a calmer, more durable love. The comparison of a poem to love at first sight is striking, but not how most poems honestly strike us. Eliot is in fact offering an inexact metaphor – full of suggestion, of uplift, of vagueness. If we try to apply the metaphor to poetry, what kind of sense does it make? I suspect Eliot was less interested in saying something about poetry than about sexual love. Applied to poetry, Eliot is saying, yet again, that poetry can communicate before it is understood – or that it can exercise a powerful attraction and appeal before we fully understand it. But it isn't – as O'Brien seems to think it is – an instruction to *stay* in a state of shock. We have to go beyond terror, beyond gallery fright – the paralysing fear of not understanding.

Neither Keats nor Eliot is on Sean O'Brien's side. At first, they may sound as though they are – but they are really *faux amis*.

Joan Acocella in the *New Yorker* (7 January 2008) was reviewing a biography of Kahlil Gibran. Mary Haskell, Gibran's sponsor, 'was so impressed by his poetry that she fell in love with him – even though it was written in Arabic – and she didn't understand Arabic'. This is an extreme, comic case of poetry communicating before it is understood. Eliot's famous dictum is in any case worthless. He says that great poetry can *sometimes* communicate before it is understood. First, communication is impossible without understanding. Second, Eliot says this is only a positive test, not a negative test. In other words, some great poetry can communicate before it is understood. Equally, great poetry sometimes may not communicate before it is understood. So, not a particularly useful criterion. Imagine it were a pregnancy test. Sometimes you can guess you're pregnant if you are pregnant, but sometimes not.

What makes a bad metaphor? Metaphor which is vague, metaphor which is pedantic, metaphor which is slow. Here are some examples.

Joseph Brodsky's essay on Derek Walcott singles out for approval *Another Life* (1973): 'A fish plops. Making rings / that marry the wide harbour'. What does marrying the harbour *mean*? Nothing. This is an example of metaphor as the instrument of vagueness, not of clarification. Compare 'Store Boy' in *The Fortunate Traveller*:

> On fading sand I pass
> a mackerel that leapt from its element,
> trying to be different –
> its eye a golden ring,
> married to nothing.

Actually this does make sense: it says that ambition to escape your given life – as store boy – results in deracination, being cut off from your roots, married to nothing.

The metaphoric impulse is bad when it is emptily gestural, semantically empty: for example, the Walcott trope equating the seagull with a hinge: viz: 'Day pivoted on a seagull's screeching hinge' (*Another Life*, Chapter 17); 'night pivots on a seagull's rusted winch' (Chapter 11); 'heard the gray, iron harbor / open on a seagull's rusty hinge' (Chapter 4, 'The Pact'). The seagull's cry and the seagull's wing beat have – apparently – a crucial but hitherto overlooked executive role in the temporal transitions during the average day. Night and day seem to require its assistance.

I don't know whether the metaphor that comes with assembly instructions isn't more comical. In Walcott's poetry, there is a recurrent equation of shining stars and shiny nails. Obvious enough, you might think. But Walcott leaves nothing to chance: ('The Schooner *Flight*') 'nail holes of stars *in the sky roof* [my italics]; (*Another Life*) 'the usual smoky twilight / blackened our galvanised roof with its nail holes of stars.'

This is Heaney in 'The Gravel Walks' in *The Spirit Level*: 'River gravel. In the beginning, that. / High summer, and the angler's motorbike / Deep in roadside flowers, like a fallen knight [so far, so *brilliant*, then comes the 'justification'] *Whose ghost we'd lately questioned:, "Any luck?"'* [my italics]. The poet doesn't trust his reader. He is officious, laborious, otiose, a line too far.

We can see similar ineptitude in Walcott's toiling equations here in *Omeros*:

> The lights stuttered in the windows,
> along the empty beach, red and green lights tossed on
> the cold harbour, and beyond them, like dominoes
> *with lights for holes*, the black skyscrapers of Boston.
>      [my italics]

Even Shakespeare isn't immune. In one of several laborious plot reprises, Edgar, in *King Lear*, tells the fatally wounded Edmund and the curious Albany how, disguised as Poor Tom O'Bedlam, he encountered the blinded Gloucester, his father: 'Met I my father with his bleeding rings, / Their precious stones new lost.' Those 'bleeding rings' would have been perfect, were it not for the pedantic insistence on expounding the metaphor: 'Their precious stones new lost.' Ah, *those* rings. Not circles, but jewellery.

This is Julian Barnes in *Nothing to Be Frightened Of*: 'Manhattan mocked by the packed verticality of the headstones.' He is passing a cemetery. Why not the cemetery's miniature Manhattan? Or 'Manhattan mocked by the headstones'? Or Allen Ginsberg's 'citylike miniature eternity' in 'At Apollinaire's Grave'. (Who would have thought Ginsberg could be economical?) Instead of this, fatal fussiness ('packed verticality') and argufying (that spurious mockery). Economy, speed, is essential to effective metaphor. It won't work if you need an identity parade, six affidavits, a recently paid utility bill and a current driving licence.

Contrast Ian McEwan, describing San Michele in *The Comfort of Strangers*: 'At this distance, the perspective distorted by a bluish early morning mist, the bright mausoleums and headstones presented the appearance of an overdeveloped city of the future.' Or Julie Maxwell's *These Are Our Children*: 'finally walk by the high-gloss obelisks of the new burial plots, a miniature Chicago of the dead'.

Now, Isaac Babel: the melodrama of the sun 'rolling across the sky like a severed head'. This is actually a semi-reminiscence of Mayakovsky's 'A Cloud in Trousers':

> The sun, like Salome,
> will dance a thousand times
> round the earth – the Baptist's head.
> (tr. Max Hayward)

Mayakovsky specialises in Big Soup, sometimes successfully:

> Do you see –
> the sky is Judas once again,
> clutching in his hand a few treacherous stars.
> (tr. James Womack)

Or:

> Again in song I glorify
> men as crumpled as hospital beds,
> and women as battered as proverbs.
> (tr. Max Hayward)

When it works, this kind of metaphor, confident in the justice of its far-fetchedness, is boldly assertive. No fidgety explanations, not one footnote about the thirty pieces of silver.

The need for economy.

The need for speed.

In *How Fiction Works*, James Wood puzzles away in the chapter on detail at why he likes Bellow's detail but dislikes that of Nabokov (and Nabokov's admirer, Updike): 'Bellow notices superbly; but Nabokov wants to tell us how important it is to notice. Nabokov's fiction is always becoming propaganda on behalf of good noticing, hence on behalf of itself.' This is misdescribed – a hastily improvised, superficially plausible reason, but it is wrong. For a start, Nabokov can be superb and the equal of Bellow. 'The tennis court was a region of great lakes' is our touchstone. But we could supply other examples without troubling to ransack the Nabokov *oeuvre*. 'Rolling the words on my tongue with the glazed-eye solemnity of a tea-taster'. '... at the last second, she surrenders her bulk to the wicker armchair, which, out of sheer fright, bursts into a salvo of crackling.' The governess's candle: 'a groggy flame squirms and ducks'. '... that flat, fallow leaf (the first casualty of the season) pasted upon a wet garden bench!' All from *Speak, Memory*.

It's perhaps worth noting that James Wood is always uneasy in the presence of writing that is so brilliant it requires only quotation and somehow renders the critic (aka James Wood) redundant – even in the case of Bellow. In his introduction to Bellow's short stories, Wood mounts a thin case for the *universality* of Bellow's detail, importing a (for Wood) saving abstract quality into Bellow's unalterably concrete specifics.

And yet, I agree with Wood's verdict on his chosen examples in *How Fiction Works*. It is the explanation which misses the mark. His first example is from Nabokov's short story 'First Love': 'an elderly flower-girl, with carbon eyebrows and a painted smile, nimbly slipped the plump torus of a carnation into the buttonhole of an intercepted stroller whose left jowl accentuated its royal fold as he glanced downward sideways at the coy insertion of the flower'. The second example is Updike on rain from *Of the Farm*: 'Its panes were strewn with drops that as if by amoebic decision would abruptly merge and break and jerkily run downward, and the window screen, like a sampler half-stitched, or a crossword puzzle invisibly solved, was inlaid erratically with minute, translucent tesserae of rain.'

Neither passage is good. But neither passage fails because it is 'propaganda on behalf of good noticing' – Wood's disguised way of agreeing with the dunces who dismiss 'writing' as showing-off. The two passages fail because they are laboured, ponderous, toiling. The former English rugby captain Will Carling was so muscle-bound he was unable to cross his legs. These sentences can't cross their legs.

Let Elizabeth Bishop explain. She is writing about Marianne Moore in 1948:

> I do not understand the nature of the satisfaction a com-pletely accurate description or imitation of anything at all can give, but apparently in order to produce it *the descrip-tion or imitation must be brief, or compact, and have at least the effect of being spontaneous.* Even the best *trompe-l'oeil* paintings lack it, but I have experienced it in listening to the noise made by a four-year-old child who could imitate exactly the sound of water running out of his bath. Long, fine, thorough passages of descriptive prose fail to produce it... [my italics]

And Elizabeth Bishop's example of a swift, 'spontaneous', suc-cessful metaphor? Marianne Moore's butterfly that 'flies off / diminishing like wreckage on the sea, / rising and falling easily'. You might equally cite Ted Hughes's *Moortown Diary* poem, 'Snow smoking as the fields boil': 'The farm-roofs sink in the welter again, like a whale's fluke.'

In his 1936 essay 'Milton I', T. S. Eliot smiled at Henry James 'painfully explaining'. Pope, in the *Dunciad Variorum* (Book I), mocked scholiasts who 'explain a thing till all men doubt it, / And write about it, Goddess, and about it'. Explanation – a thing to be avoided in metaphor. It doesn't work if you have to wind it up and consult the instruction manual.

# Chapter Seven

## *Sub-text*

Sub-text: children, when they are being scolded, can look you in the eye without making eye contact. Their pupils are black holes – withheld, absent. All parents will have encountered this. There is an equally recognisable equivalent in poetry. When a poem avoids your eye while looking straight at you, you know there is more to it than meets the eye.

Two examples from Whitman – 'Sparkles from the Wheel' and 'The Torch'. These are two straightforward poems, whose meaning is perfectly available to even the unsophisticated reader. Here is 'The Torch' in its four-line entirety:

> On my Northwest coast in the midst of the night a fisher-
> men's group stands watching,
> Out on the lake that expands before them, others are
> spearing salmon,
> The canoe, a dim shadowy thing, moves across the black
> water,
> Bearing a torch ablaze at the prow.

Why the torch? So that the fisherman can see the salmon to spear them. Perhaps to attract the fish in the first place. Is that all? I don't think so. I think Whitman is offering us an emblem of consciousness, the blaze of being, bright yet brief, in the surrounding darkness. How do I know this? I 'know' it because the poem itself sedulously refuses to pose a question, frame a conclusion. It offers a striking snapshot and stops. The feel is of something broken off, bitten back, a kind of poetic *occultatio*, the rhetorical figure that gestures towards something by looking away.

'Sparkles from the Wheel' describes a knife-grinder generating sparks from his grindstone. Again, it is a simple poem which has so little design on us (in Keats's phrase) that its advertised simplicity alerts us to the design. On the one hand, Whitman notes the grinder's distinguishing details – 'the sad sharp-chinn'd old man' – and his own spectral presence – 'effusing and fluid, a phantom':

> Where the city's ceaseless crowd moves on the livelong
> day,
> Withdrawn I join a group of children watching, I pause
> aside with them.
>
> By the curb toward the edge of the flagging,
> A knife-grinder works at his wheel sharpening a great
> knife,
> Bending over he carefully holds it to the stone, by foot and
> knee,
> With measur'd tread he turns rapidly, as he presses with
> light but firm hand,
> Forth issue then in copious golden jets,
> Sparkles from the wheel.
>
> The scene and all its belongings, how they seize and affect
> me,
> The sad sharp-chinn'd old man with worn clothes and

broad shoulder-band of leather,
Myself effusing and fluid, a phantom curiously floating,
    now here absorb'd and arrested,
The group, (an unminded point set in a vast surrounding,)
The attentive, quiet children, the loud, proud, restive base
    of the streets,
The low hoarse purr of the whirling stone, the light-
    press'd blade,
Diffusing, dropping, sideways-darting, in tiny showers of
    gold,
Sparkles from the wheel.

Even at a first reading, we are aware that this commonplace scene is imbued with something special, something rare: 'The scene and all its belongings, how they seize and affect me.' But no explanation is volunteered for Whitman's alert raptness. It might be a Wordsworthian spot of time – not exactly the inexplicable 'visionary dreariness', Wordsworth's memorable, striking paradox, but something more like the ordinary tinged with transcendence. There is a cliché in the first line, 'the livelong day', but it is redeemed because Whitman, the phantom observer, has withdrawn from it. And though he is explicitly with a group of children, he is also metaphorically at the edge of things. A liminal figure, a kind of ghost. The noun 'sparkles' sheds significance, too. It insists on literalness, on materiality. At the same time, 'sparkles' summons the noun 'spark'. We might think of Arnold's 'The Scholar-Gipsy': 'Thou waitest for the spark from Heaven.' Or we might simply see the spark as a commonplace emblem of the kindled, curtailed life.

The two poems share a vision and an idea. But they work differently. 'The Torch' plays on its own brevity, four lines only, as if the poem were a photograph cropped for significance.

We are made to focus on so little so that we will find what is hidden there – the equation of the torch and man's brief blaze. In the second, the repetition, the mild insistence, the near prolixity mask the significance of the equation – because Whitman wants to say, in addition to the equation of spark and the brevity of human existence, that the stream of transience is untroubled and endless.

★ ★ ★

Rembrandt has a double portrait of 1641, *Mennonite Preacher Anslo and his Wife*. You can see it in the Gemäldegalerie in Berlin. The preacher, in his black hat and fur-trimmed coat, is emphatically gesturing with his left hand, while he explains something to his wife. She is holding a handkerchief in her left hand on her lap and looking, not at her husband, but at three books piled on top of each other on a table. The wings of her nostrils are glazed pink. She isn't a well woman. To the left of the preacher, there is a candle stand: in one holder, a candle; in the other, smoke from a recently guttered candle. We sense a symbolic inference here. Spatially, the preacher and his wife are in the same ratio. He towers above her. The extinguished candle is proleptic. She is not long for this world.

The picture, as well as being a memento mori, is also about its own interpretation – about the way we interpret art. It addresses our intuitive conviction that meaning is hidden, deliberately concealed, in a work of art. The book on top is open, but it rests on a second book, which in turn rests on a third book, whose back is ripped off so the binding and the signatures show. All three books rest on a carpet covering a tablecloth. Of the table, we see only part of one leg.

Anslo is an adept, an expert, a professional, a sifter of arcana. There is a kind of literary criticism which is an infinite regress of prior literature. In *Axel's Castle*, Edmund Wilson sends up T. S. Eliot's learned manner in this parody of his method:

> We find this quality occasionally in Wordsworth... but it is a quality which Wordsworth shares with Shenstone rather than with Collins and Gray. And for the right sort of enjoyment of Shenstone, we must read his prose as well as his verse. The 'Essays on Men and Manners' are in the tradition of the great French aphorists of the seventeenth century, and should be read with the full sense of their relation to Vauvenargues, La Rochefoucauld, and (with his wider range) La Bruyère.

But why bother with the parody? This is Eliot *in propria persona* in 'Dante':

> But I do not wish to be thought to claim a universality for Dante which I deny to Shakespeare or Molière or Sophocles. Dante is no more 'universal' than Shakespeare: though I feel that we come nearer to understanding Dante than a foreigner can come to understanding those others. Shakespeare, or even Sophocles, or even Racine and Molière, are dealing with what is as universally human as the material of Dante; but they had no choice but to deal with it in a more local way. As I have said, the Italian of Dante is very near in feeling to medieval Latin: and of the medieval philosophers whom Dante read, and who were read by learned men of his time, there were, for instance, St Thomas who was an Italian, St Thomas's predecessor Albertus, who was a German, Abelard who was French, and Hugh and Richard of St Victor who were Scots.

Academic literary scholar-critics are similarly persuaded that literature requires their specialised knowledge for a true understanding. It is a locked house that can be opened only by specialist keys. As if writers were writing only for the cryptographer, the trained safe-cracker – a suicidal choice. 'The Sisters', the opening story of *Dubliners*, is an unsentimental look at the young, ungrateful protégé of a dead priest – a youth with a breathtaking lack of emotional affect. We expect sadness, perhaps, but instead Joyce gives us cold curiosity. The narrator is mesmerised by the word 'paralysis' – he longs 'to look upon its deadly work' – as he is struck by the word 'gnomon' in geometry. The meaning of Joyce's story is not unlocked by the technical meaning of the word 'gnomon'. The meaning is unlocked in the way the protagonist equates the word 'paralysis' not with the priest's human fate, but with the mysterious charisma of the word 'gnomon', available only to the initiate. Not mourning, then, but initiation is on the boy's mind. Where we might expect to discover innocence, Joyce gives us the craving for experience.

Mallarmé despised the bourgeoisie, who thought, because they could read, that they could read *his* poetry. But Mallarmé is an exception. So is Velimir Khlebnikov, whose poetic drama *Zangezi* is written in an invented language of gods and birds. Most writers write for intelligent readers. They want to be understood. Even if only eventually.

For instance, Joyce agonised over whether to disclose the Homeric programme under the primary narrative of *Ulysses* – finally releasing the Linati schema, with its ground-plan of organs, technics, colours and Homeric episodes. Then regretting it, according to Vladimir Nabokov, since it created the impression that the sub-text was of more importance than the main text. As if *Ulysses* were *really* about the Homeric parallels rather than the story of Leopold and Molly Bloom. Actually, it is a subtle harmonic variant on the main melody. After a bit, we can hear that the solo is a sort of duet.

Eliot is another figure who seems to lend support to the centrality of the academic specialist as the general reader's obstetrician. He candidly espouses difficulty in his essay on the metaphysical poets: 'We can only say that it appears likely that poets in our civilisation, as it exists at present, must be *difficult*.' The notes to *The Waste Land* look like an open invitation to adepts, professionals – a discouragement to amateurs without an accredited guide. And yet Eliot's meanings have proved to be *en plein vu*, in the middle of groomed slopes rather than off-piste and under a snow-job.

We never ask of natural phenomena the question we always ask of art – what does it mean? A sunset, a tree, a bird, for example. Meaning is a man-made concept. We are hard-wired for meaning. Until the question is answered, we feel uncomfortable, as Eliot noted in *The Use of Poetry*. I cite his critical touchstone again: 'The chief use of the "meaning" of a poem, in the ordinary sense, may be... to satisfy one habit of the reader, to keep his mind diverted and quiet, while the poem does its work upon him: much as the imaginary burglar is always provided with a bit of nice meat for the house-dog.' Let's be clear: Eliot is saying that the meaning of a poem, what gives it value – language, rhythm, metaphor, form – extends beyond the usual meaning of 'meaning'. Fair enough. However, the residual, primary sense of 'meaning' remains. It is a habit of mind. It is a profound, ineradicable instinct of human readers.

Here is Robert Frost writing to William Stanley Braithwaite, an African-American poet-critic, on 22 March 1915. Frost begins with a distinction between real life and art, and his belief that art involves the imposition of meaning on raw experience. 'A story must always release a meaning more readily to those who read than life itself as it goes ever releases meaning.'

A sunset in real life has no meaning, so to speak, whereas a sunset in a story or a poem has. Here is Eliot's 'Portrait of A Lady': '"Yet with these April sunsets, that somehow recall / My buried life, and Paris in the Spring…"' The woman speaker invokes the sunsets as a sentimental synecdoche for her past romantic life, a burden of solipsistic meaning a sunset cannot objectively support. At the end of the poem, the male speaker refers not to 'sunsets', but to a particular sunset on the day the woman might die, 'Afternoon grey and smoky, *evening yellow and rose*' [my italics]. A specific sunset, then, distinguished from the generic with its sentimental charge – the generic as we encounter it in 'The Love Song of J. Alfred Prufrock': 'After the sunsets and the dooryards and the sprinkled streets', a list in which the items move away from the broadly evocative to the particular 'sprinkled streets' and 'the skirts that trail along the floor'. Prufrock the romantic edged by Eliot the poet into painful particulars. Just as when, evoking *mermaids*, Eliot gives his protagonist recourse to 'seaweed red and brown', to actual seaweed.

Frost is clear about one thing we should also be clear about: 'Meaning is a great consideration.' Then he adds that this necessary meaning must be disguised. 'But a story must never seem to be told primarily for meaning. Anything, an inspired irrelevancy even to make it sound as if told the way it is chiefly because it happened that way.' There is always a negotiation between meaning and blatancy. As Keats said, we hate poetry with a palpable design on us. All three poets, Eliot, Frost and Keats, want to give meaning its proper value and to put it in its place – to argue the importance of form as well as content. All three are against the tendentious, the obvious, the moralising.

A poet like Miroslav Holub was compelled to disguise his meaning for political reasons. The curious thing to me is that the disguises he used are transparent, not in the least difficult to decipher. When he writes a poem called 'Polonius' and sets Polonius behind an arras, we know immediately that the poem is about a secret policeman or an informer to the secret police. Presumably, the secret police knew this immediately too, being politically educated and ideologically attuned to the strategies, the obliquities, of dissent.

There is a Russian joke about dissent. A man walks through Red Square, shouting at the top of his voice that there are no food shortages in Russia, that elections are above reproach, that there is freedom of speech. He is arrested almost immediately. 'What did I say that was wrong?' he asks the police. Their answer: 'We know what you mean.'

The protection afforded Holub is deniability. Or, rather, unprovability. The obvious equation – between Polonius and the spy – is never stated directly. The equation is left to the reader to complete. The sub-text is compellingly summoned, not by the text itself, but by the context – the political conditions in Czechoslovakia, which are outside the text.

The Holub poem is a special case of sub-text – intended by the author but only confirmed by political context. It is closer to Jan Kott's *Shakepeare Our Contemporary* than to a pure sub-text. Kott's *Hamlet*, for instance, helplessly reflected political conditions on the ground in Poland. (And Nicholas Hytner's *Hamlet* at the National Theatre in 2010 had Patrick Malahide's brilliant Claudius surrounded by secret service agents in suits listening to their ear-pieces: a contrived, deliberate, but highly effective reading of the play, imposed by the director, not by the audience with the collusion of the director. This isn't a sub-text, but an *over-text*.) Kott's reading of *Richard III* was yet another reflection of realpolitik, refracted through Shakespeare.

In the case of Jan Kott, the author is innocent, the sub-text is imposed from without. Normal sub-text is intentional and authorial. We recognise its presence *by surface enigma*. Or sub-text feels required *by surface thinness* – a flagrant insufficiency about what is apparently on offer.

It is always possible to imagine a sub-text where none exists, to import the critic's own agenda into the poem. Eliot's figure for this in 'The Function of Criticism' is the surgeon whose pockets are full of body parts, which he intends to smuggle into the cadaver. This is Tom Paulin's preferred methodology. He is so persuaded of the importance of politics that he cannot believe trace elements of political issues are not encrypted in every text. In Kipling's story 'Mary Postgate' – a dark narrative decidedly athwart the Beerbohm caricature – Paulin found the tritest reflection of British imperialism as outwardly civilised but internally barbaric. The spinster who derives sexual pleasure from the death of an enemy airman is, for Paulin, a coarse allegory of the British Empire. It seems not to occur to him that the imperialist Kipling might not wish to portray the British Empire in this incriminating way. In any case, Kipling's story has nothing to do with British imperialism. Paulin is like a policeman placing a brick into Kipling's pocket and then charging him with possession of an offensive weapon.

In *Minotaur*, Paulin misreads Larkin's poem 'Afternoons' in exactly the same way.

> Summer is fading:
> The leaves fall in ones and twos
> From trees bordering
> The new recreation ground.
> In the hollows of afternoons

Young mothers assemble
At swing and sandpit
Setting free their children.

Behind them, at intervals,
Stand husbands in skilled trades,
An estateful of washing,
And the albums, lettered
*Our Wedding*, lying
Near the television:
Before them, the wind
Is ruining their courting-places

That are still courting-places
(But the lovers are all in school),
And their children, so intent on
Finding more unripe acorns,
Expect to be taken home.
Their beauty has thickened.
Something is pushing them
To the side of their own lives.

This, too, according to Paulin, is 'about' the British Empire –
rather than a poem about the gradual diminished sense of self
that accrues with age. Leaves fall, for instance, 'rather like colon-
ies dropping out of the empire'. Mothers are pushed to the side
of their lives – 'a metaphor for a sense of diminished purpose
and fading imperial power'. You begin to wonder, after even a
short time spent in Paulin's company, whether everything isn't
a disguised version of the British Empire. That woman pushing
a pram, for instance, is probably working for MI5 and the pram
is her cover.

Actually, Paulin isn't entirely fixated on the Empire. His reading of Coleridge's 'Frost at Midnight' is another perverse masterpiece:

> ...whether the eave-drops fall
> Heard only in the trances of the blast,
> Or if the secret ministry of frost
> Shall hang them up in silent icicles,
> Quietly shining to the quiet Moon.

Coleridge's poem was written in February 1798. Paulin: 'In this violent context, the images of icicles hanging – being hung up – under the eaves can seem strangely proleptic.' Proleptic of what? In Paulin's account of the poem, proleptic of a French invasion of England and summary revolutionary justice for aristocrats. You might think this is a long way from a poet thinking about icicles. Paulin, however, sees a play on 'ministry' – a word with political as well as spiritual connotations. You might even think that, far from being proleptic, it is a retrospective look at the excesses of the French Revolution. There's a lot of hypothesis in Paulin's reading – an invasion, for a start, and then a French victory. It is true that Coleridge was, in later years, persuaded that Napoleon had his name on a death-list. But Paulin is proposing not paranoia, the vanity of authorship and the self-importance of journalists, but an actual historical possibility – French revolutionary justice, Madame Guillotine at Marble Arch. Except, by St George, the guillotine will evidently be supplanted by hanging – Moll Flanders's 'the steps and the string' – as a concession to British custom, a ploy to get the conservative populace on side.

The quiet tone of 'Frost at Midnight' is a problem for

Paulin's bloodthirsty interpretation. He draws in his stomach and eases past it, barely disturbing it – or himself. 'This is a language that aspires to an innocence it cannot acquire.' Where does Coleridge stand in relation to this sentence? Is Coleridge saying, don't be fooled by my tone and my diction? Or is Coleridge saying, I'm trying to put the best face on this, but fear keeps showing through the cosmetic presentation? Does Paulin think the sub-text is intended or involuntary? He doesn't say. He doesn't say because he cannot know. Perhaps the unregenerate Marxist in him thinks that history is actually the author of this poem – of all poems. Edward Said reads *Mansfield Park* in the light cast by Sir Thomas Bertram's commercial interests in the sugar plantations and therefore slavery. Said knows (and concedes) that he is distorting the perspective of the novel, deliberately bending it to his own political interests. Paulin gives us no comparable unrepentant indication that he knows his readings are skewed.

Academic criticism – part of the moralistic Leavisite legacy, perhaps – has an equally pronounced characteristic squint. Not the predetermined discovery of a political residuum – Paulin's strabismus, as *that* is known – but a disposition to empty abstraction and its attractive 'philosophical' acoustic. On 1 October 1972, Tom Stoppard initiated a series in the *Times Literary Supplement* called 'Doers and Thinkers'. This first essay (and the last, as it proved) was entitled 'Playwrights and Professors' and focused on Ibsen's *Ghosts*. Stoppard quotes Professor Richard Gilman on *Ghosts*: 'The real subject of *Ghosts*, for example, is surely not "the rigidity of middleclass Norwegian morality", as a recent critic (Lionel Abel), thinking no doubt to get past the *flagrant insufficiency* [my italics] of venereal disease as a theme, has found it possible to argue.' Professor Gilman has a different and to him more plausible theme: '*Ghosts* is "about" something far less fettered to an era or a locality: it is about the rigidities, the fatal blind movements of ideals and abstractions in a universe of facts.' (I love the apologetic inverted commas around 'about'.)

This is Stoppard's pragmatic and exasperated response to Professor Gilman: 'Now to begin with, *Ghosts* is "about" venereal disease. That is to say, it is about particular people in a particular situation. That's the level on which a play lives or dies. If Ibsen had set out to write about the blind movements of ideals and abstractions in a universe of fact, his chances of immortality would have been roughly the same as the average critic's.' Stoppard has identified a critical tic – the instinct, the impulse, to eliminate the concrete, as if life itself was a little low-life, and replace it with a pros*thesis*. As it might be, the problem of identity, the role of history, the failure of communication, the isolation of the individual, or any of the other nursery notions that critics clutch at for comfort.

Richard Gilman is wrong about *Ghosts*. But he articulates a useful method, even as he misuses it, of identifying the possible presence of a sub-text – viz: 'the flagrant insufficiency' of what is ostensibly on offer. In prose, it is often more easily identifiable. A story like Hemingway's 'Big Two-Hearted River' is a perfect illustration of Hemingway's tip of the iceberg theory – the story will be strengthened by what has been eliminated. Kipling in *Something of Myself* deployed a similar narrative economy and described the process as analogous to riddling a fire until only the hottest coals were left. Hemingway's narrative is extended, meticulous, and finally, subtly evasive as the details of Nick's fishing trip accumulate to no evident purpose. Can this be all? is the question that poses itself. And we are gradually made aware that the story is about the trauma of war. Pinter uses the same technique in his early plays, where extended exchanges of banalities are prolonged until they create comedy or menace – or both.

## Ivesian Fugue

The string quartet
at our fête champêtre
revealed such fierce sonorities –
*Bonk, bonk, bonk!* –
that I stopped to consider
how music springs from catgut,
and four men bobbing
and scuttling on a lawn.

Christopher Reid's poem 'Ivesian Fugue' appears to be a description of a string quartet playing outdoors – playing something strenuously modern. The sound relayed to us by the poet is '*bonk, bonk, bonk*'. In fact, this is a classic Martian poem, which follows the symbolist method of Mallarmé as outlined in his famous letter to Henri Cazalis: '*peindre non la chose, mais l'effet qu'elle produit*' [don't paint the thing; paint the effect produced by the thing]. The thing has to be deduced from its effects '*par une série de déchiffrements*' [by a series of decipherings]. The effect here is the illusion of a string quartet playing testing, radical music. The thing itself, which has to be deduced, is a doubles tennis match. (Christopher Reid's inspiration may have come from Debussy's *Jeux*, which is based on tennis players.) The pleasure of the poem lies in the deft dual application of everything described: four people 'bobbing' and 'scuttling' is an evocation of the half-dancing, the quarter-Tourette's, of musicians putting their backs into making music – and their arms and their legs and (above all) their heads. How do we know to look further than the given string quartet? 'Bobbing' is exact enough for a quartet, but 'scuttling' is a deliberate stretch – insufficient, if not flagrantly insufficient. It is indicative without being absolutely accurate as an account of the way musicians perform music. It isn't an exact fit. It isn't an exact enough fit. There is a thinness which, if we trust the poet, is an invitation to press on through to the ordained but occluded destination – tickets to the centre court.

Saul Bellow, in *To Jerusalem and Back*, mentions an infuriating reader who interprets all his writing in political terms. He has three characters taking coffee in Chicago, Bellow complains, and the woman (yes, it isn't Tom Paulin) writes that this is the Tehran Conference with Churchill, Stalin and Roosevelt. Or the Yalta Conference. Or the Potsdam Conference. This kind of over-interpretation is common enough – for example, Christopher Bigsby on Edward Albee's *Who's Afraid of Virginia Woolf*. The central characters are called George and Martha, Christian names they share with George Washington and his wife. Ergo, Albee's play is a play about America. This is Bigsby's programme note for an Almeida Theatre production: 'beyond its excoriating portrait of a marriage sustained and enlivened by fantasy, and the brilliant but wounding articulacy of both participants, [it] offers a portrait of America as deeply uncommunal, morally equivocal and self-deluding.' This interpretation satisfies two sublimated desires at once: it addresses the anti-Americanism endemic in left-wing politics; and it demonstrates the superior sagacity of the professional academic reader, who is able to uncover a facet of the play invisible to the amateur reader.

Bigsby is mistaken. The references to Spengler's *The Decline of the West*, which are crucial to the argument he wishes to make about America's terminal decline, are not seeded by the playwright as clues to an allegorical reading of the play. They are references *in character*, restricted to George, specific to George – who is a professional historian, applying Spengler's ideas of 'goddam historical inevitability' to personal relations, not to America. George can see that, *mutatis mutandis*, the young couple Nick and Honey are going to change into the older couple. They have already had a phantom pregnancy which 'repeats' the fantasy son of George and Martha. George originally planned to take over the history department. He failed. We can see that Nick, who has similar plans in the biology department, will fail too.

Bigsby's allegorical reading of the play arises from the fatal sense that venereal disease, marital torment, love and betrayal are flagrantly insufficient as subjects. In a Spenglerian way, Professor Bigsby has inherited the gorgeous but imaginary mantle of Richard Gilman.

How do we differentiate between an inviting thinness and hubristic imposition? There is no rule, no reliable test. There are broad guidelines, as I have explained. In the end, however, like much in poetry, we are compelled to rely on experience and on intelligence. How do you distinguish between the calculated thinness of Christopher Reid's 'Ivesian Fugue' and the total sufficiency of *Who's Afraid of Virginia Woolf?* By having taste, by having a *feel* for what is likely, by an ability to read. I stand with T. S. Eliot, who wrote in 'The Perfect Critic' in *The Sacred Wood*: 'in his short and broken treatise [Aristotle] provides an eternal example – not of laws, or even of method, for there is no method except to be very intelligent...'

## Some Examples of Sub-text

'Whose woods these are I think I know.' Frost's 'Stopping by Woods on a Snowy Evening' begins with an inversion which is completely naturalised by the vernacular:

> Whose woods these are I think I know.
> His house is in the village though;
> He will not see me stopping here
> To watch his woods fill up with snow.

Everything in this poem depends on the vernacular. The rhyme scheme is a kind of terza rima – except that everything is rhymed four times: here/queer/near/year. (There are two exceptions: the first rhyme sounds only three times and the last is five times.) There is a mimetic effect here: the rhyme stands still; it doesn't move on. It lingers like the speaker.

The thrust of the poem is that Frost stops to observe the beauty for aesthetic reasons. His horse, accustomed to utilitarian purpose, is puzzled. The impulse to aesthetic pleasure is set against practicality – and practicality triumphs. The woods are 'lovely' but Frost has duties and commissions ('promises to keep') and he is still a long way from home and bed ('miles to go before I sleep').

And the sub-text? Its presence is signalled by the final repetition of 'And miles to go before I sleep'. True, Frost's design on his reader is sheltered by the naturalness of this repetition, its plausible vernacular. Nevertheless, the familiar equation of death with its euphemism 'sleep' – he sleeps with the angels – exerts its subtle pressure. And the meaning of the poem shifts. 'The woods are lovely, dark and deep' suggests not only beauty but disappearance into the darkness of death and the deepness of the grave. We recall the Keats who is 'half in love with easeful Death' – the Keats who, in 'Ode to the Nightingale', imagines himself deep in a wood, in 'embalmèd darkness'. The adjective 'embalmèd' is significant. Frost's second conclusion, his sub-textual conclusion, is that death looks attractive, restful

– compare Ralph Touchett in James's *Portrait of a Lady*: 'What does it matter if I'm tired when I have all eternity to rest?' But however attractive the idea of rest is, life has to be lived. 'And miles to go before I sleep.'

Frost's 'A Patch of Old Snow' looks like a poem about a bit of visual misprision, mistaking a patch of snow for an old newspaper. This would be slight, but not impossible as the subject for a poem. What is interesting is that – in a poem that begins with an admission of the mistake – Frost, in the final two lines, treats the newspaper as if it were real. The grimy snow is speckled with dirt like a newspaper speckled with print – *print with news Frost has forgotten, if he ever read it*. The snow isn't *like* a newspaper. It *is* an old newspaper. Frost treats it as a reality to which he is indifferent, with a kind of doughty impatience and offhand hostility. The mood is like that conjured up by William Carlos Williams's 'The Last Words of My English Grandmother' as the grandmother looks out of the ambulance window:

> What are all those
> fuzzy-looking things out there?
> Trees? Well, I'm tired
> of them and rolled her head away.

It is the persistence in the mistake – in the confusion of newspaper and old snow – that signals to the reader that we are listening to an old person, cantankerously overriding his own correction. This in turn makes the sub-text clear – that the patch of old snow is a figure for the old who might feel they have outlived their time and are persisting, anomalous as that patch of old snow.

Frost's 'Good Hours' is a poem in the same area as 'A Patch of Old Snow'. The speaker recounts going for a walk in the winter evening alone. He walks to the edge of the village through the snow, seeing human activity through the windows of the houses. On his return journey, every window is black, the people asleep. One word alerts the reader to the sub-text – 'Over the snow my creaking feet / Disturbed the slumbering village street / Like *profanation*...' The word could be explained as hyperbole – disturbing the peace – except that Frost specifies the early hour of ten o'clock. The word sends us back into the poem. The first line – 'I had for my winter evening walk' – is a plausible, muted figure for old age. Frost then deploys a ghost topos: his returning self is a revenant and that is why he is a 'profanation'. Not a literal ghost, just a person without substance, cut off from human activity, one of the old, one of the functionally invisible.

'Good Hours' and 'A Patch of Old Snow' work on the same sub-textual principle – a surface 'inadequacy' that prompts further searching. 'Now Close the Windows' uses the sub-textual principle of enigma. The poem issues commands – a little like Auden's 'Stop all the clocks' – but resolutely thwarts our curiosity about the motivation for those commands. Why does the speaker desire quiet? 'Now close the windows and hush all the fields; / If the trees must, let them silently toss...' The fourth line is a clue. No bird is singing – 'and if there is, / Be it my loss.' The word 'loss' suggests, I think, something more than the immediate sense, which is that the speaker accepts the consequence of his decision to close the windows. The sub-text is that his loss is singing. He is absorbed in listening to his loss and does not want to be distracted. The second stanza offers us the uncontroversial idea that it will be some time before morning – 'It will be long ere the marshes resume, / It will be long ere the earliest bird' – but there is something in the repetition that suggests a greater dimension. In fact, a long dark *night* of the soul, a lengthy encounter with grief, before the speaker can rejoin the world. He is cut off – as the world is cut off from him by design.

Now, two poems by Simon Armitage whose sub-text is sex – 'Very Simply Topping up the Brake Fluid' and 'Never Mind the Quality:'. 'Very Simply' brilliantly captures the voice of the garage mechanic-proprietor, its authentic fluency, its casual authority, its technical vocabulary ('the spade connector', 'the float-chamber', 'the clutch reservoir') – all within an invisible rhyme scheme of abba ('pour', 'spill it, it's', 'fill it till it's', 'reservoir'). Never has enjambement seemed more natural, more necessary or apt. The voice is at ease with itself, self-confident and confidently set down by Armitage with the quiet certainty of Kipling, the great master of dialect: 'Oh don't mind him, love, / he doesn't bite. Come here and sit down Prince. Prince!' There is something in the title which nudges us in the direction of a sub-text – the qualifier, 'very simply', which suggests it isn't as simple as it seems. *Here is a man who knows what he is doing*:

> Now you're all right
>
> to unscrew, no, clockwise, you see it's Russian
> love, back to front, that's it.

But some men don't know what they are doing: 'If you want / us again we're in the book. Tell your husband.' The last three words are crucial to the sub-text. Tell your husband we're in the book. Tell your husband the piece of mechanical skill I've just shown you.

Armitage's 'Never Mind the Quality:' has an Amisian reversal of roles. Martin Amis, in his story 'Career Move', makes poets fêted pool-side in Hollywood by film moguls, while their novelist counterparts toil unrewarded. Armitage has the men in his poem wearing aprons and swilling the pavement, tied to the sink and the stove. Michael Hofmann, in an interview with David Sexton, in the early days of the *Literary Review*, described his idea of poetic form as like tearing wallpaper: it ended where its momentum ended. Just as 'Very Simply' is about efficient method, the mechanics of blake-fluid and the mechanics of the clitoris, so 'Never Mind the Quality:' is about stripping wallpaper. The woman strips a piece of wallpaper, but instead of it breaking and stopping, it goes impossibly on... The sub-text is the female's first orgasm and self-empowerment. It's about masturbation: she 'took it in hand' and it took off, 'kept coming, breathtaking...' There is also an innuendo of exaggeration, a hint that hyperbole will keep the men cowed – as the women were once cowed themselves. It is also about power in sexual politics. How do we know? We know because the narrative is nonsense, or non-sense, a tall story we need to trim to truth – a version of the enigma signalling the presence of a sub-text.

This is even more the case with Paul Muldoon's 'Cows'. The cover narrative, the faux overlay, is two drinkers al fresco, who first witness a red flashing light from the back of a truck and then hear a smoker's cough which sparks a chorus of coughing cows. Things are not what they seem. The drinkers are caught in cross-fire in bandit country. The rear light on the blink is actually the muzzle of a rifle, the coughing of the cows an exchange of fire. Tim Kendall's reading of the poem is cagily equivocal, undecided because afraid of being wrong – anxiously attentive to detail, but unwilling to look up from its crewel-work and say what the whole is about: 'What "Cows" actually records... is an incident on a dark night... in smuggling territory near the Irish border; a cattle truck is as likely to be laden with microwaves or hi-fis as with cows. Although the poem never mentions that the truck may be carrying an altogether more deadly hardware, the sudden shift of tone in its final section would suggest that such a possibility is certainly implicit...' You see? Everything and nothing. This is a reading without triage. It is fearful of committing itself to a hierarchy of importance – so the ingredients are left as they are in the poem. Everything noted, nothing explained. 'What "Cows" actually records' – wait for it – 'is an incident on a dark night.' Kendall mentions the hardware, guns, but he hasn't assembled the poem, which remains a sequence of unresolved possibilities.

Muldoon's narrator is a man of fine distinctions. He supplies the etymology of 'boreen'. He discriminates, in his finicky literary way, between 'Wellesley' and 'Wesleyan' colleges; between 'Céline and Paul Celan' – twinnings that mirror the more crucial likeness between coughing and gunshots. How easy it is to make a mistake. How important to distinguish one thing from its likeness. Failure to do so could be fatal.

# Chapter Eight

## *Poetry and Indistinctness*

John Banville (*New York Review of Books*, 15 July 2010) has retreated from his former unstinting admiration for Nabokov's prose. 'The argument could be made that stylists of the high, Nabokovian variety – of which, it should be observed, there are not many, and almost all of them male – are literary bullies in their insistence that we accept exclusively their highly polished and rigidly fixed accounts of how things are within the little rounds that their fictions create.' The famous Nabokovian precision – describing things accurately and vividly – curtails the freedom of the reader and betrays the 'brightly fluttering spontaneity' of reality, according to Banville. Those definitive phrases pre-empt the reader's approximations:

> what some deplore in Nabokov is the denial of imaginative manoeuvre, of that dreamy and delightful freedom of the reader to imagine *through* an author's style and make a world of his or her own out of the materials the writer offers. The uncanny version of things that Nabokov presents us with is, for such unenchanted readers, a wilful chloroforming and pinning down of that brightly fluttering spontaneity that is the essence of reality...

Banville evidently prefers his own bricolage. I find this preference for the unfocused wrong-headed – rather as if you dismissed Placido Domingo because you preferred hearing your own bawling arias in the bathtub.

Banville is not alone in this preference for imprecision, for indistinctness, for fog. In *What Good Are the Arts?*, one of our liveliest critics, John Carey, singles out Shakespeare as an exemplary exponent of indistinctness – verbal and metaphorical – that allows the reader to create his own work of art. The reader, Carey argues, uses his imagination to eke out the indistinct details provided by Shakespeare. Marlowe, Shakespeare's predecessor, allegedly uses simile as an instrument of clarification, of distinctness. For Carey, Marlowe's method is inferior to Shakespeare's and to post-Shakespearean writers who have profited from Shakespeare's example. (Carey isn't pedantic, though: one of his examples is taken from Marlowe.)

Carey's proposition isn't completely new. It is a variant on reader-response theory – Wolfgang Iser's idea that the reader creates the art – and also T. S. Eliot's idea that the meaning of a work of art lies somewhere between the reader and the writer. Carey, however, supplies particular examples. This is crucial. Without examples, the argument is safely abstract. Remember Eliot on Dante, shrewdly heading off the scholars? 'I mean to restrict my comments to the unprovable and the irrefutable.'

Ultimately, Carey proposes something more radical than Eliot or Iser: DIY art.

Shakespeare is not a builder so much as a builder's yard – from the raw materials he supplies, each reader will make something individual and necessarily different. Or, you might want to say, after considering Carey's analysis of particular examples, that 'demolition' might be a better word for what the reader, Carey in this case, brings to the poetry.

Naturally, Carey's liberal cast of mind means that he welcomes all these different individual readings as necessarily valid. Whereas it seems obvious to me that there are good, attentive, sensitive readers and very bad readers. In fact, I think we can look at Carey's own readings and wonder how good a reader *he* is. As I said earlier, Helen Gardner pointed out a quarter of a century ago, while attacking Empson's seven types of ambiguity, that reading involves the elimination of irrelevant meanings and suggestions which obscure the intended meaning. You can either read to make sense of what you are reading. Or you can read to make non-sense of what you are reading. Carey makes it his business to remain in a state of wilful indistinctness.

For example, he discusses Housman's 'Tell Me Not Here', a poem about 'remembered countryside pleasures', and he quotes:

> On russet floors, by waters idle,
> The pine lets fall its cone;
> The cuckoo shouts all day at nothing
> In leafy dells alone...

Not many problems here, you might think. But Carey is baffled, as if the words had suddenly become encrypted: 'A cuckoo may be in a dell but it cannot be in dells. Or is it "nothing" that is in the dells? "Dells" opens up innumerable echoing spaces around the cuckoo, spaces in which its shout is heard though it may not be actually present.' Not actually present because it can't be in more than one place at once. This is Carey's argument. Housman seems to be requiring the impossible of the cuckoo. In fact, Housman is merely saying the cuckoo goes from dell to dell shouting at nothing. Wordsworth's 'To the Cuckoo – ' will explain the idea for Professor Carey: 'O Cuckoo! shall I call thee Bird, / Or but a wandering Voice?'

POETRY AND INDISTINCTNESS · 127

What *would* be impossible, actually, is the notion that the cuckoo spends all day in the same dell. I offer this as an example of Professor Carey's sedulous perversity – his determination to read with a pedantic, inappropriate literalness, wherever possible avoiding the obvious. He is baffled on principle. Compare Terry Eagleton's notorious example of language's unreliability: a man goes up an escalator and sees a sign, 'Dogs Must be Carried on the Escalator'. Does this mean that if you have a dog you should carry it? Or does it mean that without a dog you aren't allowed on the escalator? Obviously, the first. Language isn't a failed system of communication unless you are very determined in your stupidity. Language cannot protect itself from systematic, principled idiocy.

Eagleton's example of language's semantic unreliability is a variant on the *Beyond the Fringe* sketch performed by Jonathan Miller. Miller addressed the import of the legend 'Gentlemen Lift the Seat' above British Rail toilets. Did this mean that a definition of the gentleman is someone who lifts the toilet seat before urinating? Or is it a loyal toast?

Commenting on Milton's *Comus*, Carey affects not to understand Comus's commendation of the Lady's Song: 'At every fall smoothing the raven down / Of darkness, till it smiled.' The sense of the metaphor is this: 'the song smooths the darkness until it shines – smiles – like a raven's wing.' Here is Carey making heavy weather of this simple metaphor: 'A smiling raven? Or is it "darkness" that smiles, and what would that look like?'

The image is so familiar as to be almost clichéd – the night was 'black as a raven's wing'; her hair was 'black as a raven's wing'. In Hemingway's *A Moveable Feast* there is a woman with hair as black as a crow's wing. Byron's poem 'She Walks in Beauty', celebrates 'the nameless grace / Which waves in every raven tress.'

What would smiling, shining darkness look like? Stars, of course. Compare Sylvia Plath's 'By Candlelight': there, night is 'A sort of black horsehair, / A rough, dumb country stuff / Steeled with the sheen / Of what green stars can make it to the gate.'

All metaphorical language is vulnerable to unrelenting literalism – because metaphor turns on similarity in dissimilarity, it breaches the literal. It says that two things are alike when, in many ways, they are not. All metaphor joins things that are not comparable considered rationally, Carey argues: 'Metaphor, like rhyme, is a way of connecting things contrary to reason.' This is only superficially true. Were it absolutely true, all poetry would be nonsense poetry – a statement Carey comes close to endorsing. Metaphor joins things – things which are different in several ways, in *most* ways – by a single point of similarity. As readers, most of us have no problem with identifying the just point of comparison.

William Golding, a favourite author, is a key example in Carey's argument. Ironically enough, Golding sends up unblinking literalism at the end of the first chapter of *Lord of the Flies*. Ralph, Jack and Simon have reached the top of the mountain, discovered that they are on an island, and are now beginning their descent – when they encounter 'bushes [that] were dark evergreen and aromatic and the many buds were waxen green and folded up against the light'. Simon, the mystic and poet, ventures a metaphor: '"Like candles. Candle bushes. Candle buds."' His two companions are as literal as John Carey: '"You couldn't light them. They just look like candles"' (Ralph); '"Green candles... we can't eat them"' (Jack).

Discussing *Pincher Martin*, Carey quotes Golding's matchless, vivid account of the way a grain of chocolate feels to a starving man: 'He unfolded the paper with great care: but there was nothing left inside. He put his face close to the glittering paper and squinted at it. In one crease there was a single brown grain. He put out his tongue and took the grain. The chocolate stung with a piercing sweetness, momentary and agonising, and was gone.' There is one remarkable word here: 'stung', which is counter-intuitive when sweetness is at issue. 'Agonising' is also counter-intuitive given the smallness of the 'grain'. Carey likes the passage – but, for him, it illustrates not precise imagination, but 'indistinctness': 'the actual taste of chocolate is not there.' According to Carey, the reader has to supply the taste and complete the writing. But he is misreading: the taste of the chocolate isn't there at all. There is so little chocolate that all Pincher Martin experiences is pain – not flavour. Golding is describing and imagining an experience the reader could not know about – starvation so severe that a tiny quantity of chocolate detonates on the tongue. And he imagines this with great precision, with perfect distinctness, *exactly*.

The base position here is like Ted Hughes's comment on the inadequacy of words in *Poetry in the Making*. In his afterword, Hughes is unconvinced by language's ability to cope with the sheer immediacy, the *thinginess* of the world: 'there are no words to capture the infinite depth of crowiness in the crow's flight.' He bewails the inadequacy of language – 'all we can do is use a word as an indicator, or a whole bunch of words as a general directive' – yet he demonstrates at the same time the power of words not only to equal reality, but to surpass it:

> but the ominous thing in the crow's flight, the bare-faced bandit thing, the tattered beggarly gipsy thing, the caressing and shaping yet slightly clumsy gesture of the downstroke, as if the wings were both too heavy and too powerful, and the headlong sort of merriment, the macabre pantomime

ghoulishness, and the undertaker sleekness – you could go on for a very long time with phrases of that sort and still have completely missed your instant, glimpsed knowledge of the world of the crow's wingbeat.

Even as he employs it so brilliantly, Hughes obviously under-rates the power of language. But the root misapprehension is the assumption, natural enough, that reality is real. It isn't. Most of the time, reality, as most people perceive it, is experientially impoverished. When we see a crow, for instance, we don't see it with an iota of the vividness conveyed by Hughes's phrases. Just as the word 'crow' merely denotes a particular bird, so the bird signified is merely registered in the normal course of things. We do not apprehend it. Language can do that for us, which is why we value art.

By praising the indistinctness of Shakespeare's language, Carey believes he is praising linguistic innovation. He thinks Shakespeare is doing something completely new – unlikely as that is. His argument runs like this: the signifier cannot equal the signified in the real world. It cannot be precise enough. And therefore it adopts a strategy of indistinctness. It makes a virtue of necessity and the reader is recruited to help.

This is Carey on crows in *Macbeth*:

> Light thickens, and the crow
> Makes wing to the rooky wood;
> Good things of day begin to droop and drowse,
> Whiles night's black agents to their preys do rouse…

By now you can perhaps anticipate Carey's objection – for it is really an objection, not praise. Looking for indistinctness, his objection to the poetry concerns 'night's black agents'. What are they? Do they include the crow? It is, Carey notes, going home to roost, which suggests it is harmless, but, he argues, its blackness is against it. This is wilful: if it is roosting, then it is likely to droop and drowse, and is therefore excluded from the black agents. The indistinctness is all of Carey's making. As for the black agents, they include all the night-time predators. Owls, stoats, ferrets, foxes. No mystery, no indistinctness there – only lack of specification, only the generic.

Sometimes things aren't so clear-cut in the area of indistinctness. In *Lord of the Flies*, Golding describes a kind of plankton and the way in which Simon's dead body is carried out to sea. Clare Ostle, a marine biologist, told me these are phosphorescent plankton. Golding's description of plankton is quite clear, though he doesn't specify what type of plankton it might be:

Along the shoreward edge of the shallows the advancing clearness was full of strange, moonbeam-bodied creatures with fiery eyes. *Here and there a larger pebble clung to its own air and was covered with a coat of pearls.* The tide swelled in over the *rain-pitted sand* and smoothed everything with a layer of silver. Now it touched the first of the stains that seeped from the broken body and the creatures made a moving patch of light as they gathered at the edge. The water rose further and dressed Simon's coarse hair with brightness. The line of his cheek silvered and the turn of his shoulder became sculptured marble. The strange, attendant creatures, with their fiery eyes and trailing vapours, busied themselves round his head. The body lifted a fraction of an inch from the sand and a bubble of air escaped from the mouth with a wet plop. Then it turned gently in the water.

Somewhere over the darkened curve of the world the sun and moon were pulling; and the film of water on the earth planet was held, bulging slightly on one side while the solid core turned. The great wave of tide moved further along the island and the water lifted. Softly, surrounded by a fringe of inquisitive bright creatures, itself a silver shape beneath the steadfast constellations, Simon's dead body moved out towards the open sea. [my italics]

The rain-pitted sand. *'Here and there a larger pebble clung to its own air and was covered with a coat of pearls.'* How distinct, how magnified is that, how microscopically precise. How Joycean. Joyce was a writer incapable of indistinctness.

Carey, reasonably enough, wonders what the fiery creatures are. But not enough to work out they must be the plankton. We are invited instead to observe his DIY. According to him, the creatures have teeth. Teeth are not mentioned here. They are mentioned earlier, in Chapter Four, when Golding, quite lucidly, describes these scavengers. Carey has half-remembered one detail of what he has largely forgotten. The creatures don't *have* teeth. They are *like* 'a myriad of tiny teeth in a saw'. Roger is watching Henry exercising mastery over little creatures at the sea's edge. 'There were creatures that lived in this last fling of the sea, tiny transparencies that came questing in with the water over the hot, dry sand... Like a myriad of tiny teeth in a saw, the transparencies came scavenging over the beach.'

Carey, reading the later passage, also volunteers that perhaps the creatures are merely nuzzling and nudging – not using their 'teeth'. He concludes that it is 'not spelled out either way'. In other words, he is adding unwarranted embellishments and confusion to Golding's text.

I'm not sure how Golding could have been more specific, more distinct, in his account of these quasi-angelic attendant creatures, without impairing their peculiar status, their role as ministering entities.

Had he wanted absolute distinctness, he could, of course, have described them with zoological precision. I asked Richard Dawkins what kind of plankton he thought Golding had in mind. Dawkins suggested ctenophores (or the phylum ctenophora), otherwise known as Venus's girdles. The scientific description is only distinct and clear to a zoologist:

> ctenophores, variously known as comb jellies, sea gooseberries, sea walnuts, or Venus's girdles, are voracious predators. Unlike cnidarians, with which they share several superficial similarities, they lack stinging cells. Instead, in order to capture prey, ctenophores possess sticky cells called colloblasts. In a few species, special cilia in the mouth are used for biting gelatinous prey. The phylogenetic position of the ctenophores has been and still is in dispute. Ctenophores have a pair of anal pores, which have sometimes been interpreted as homologous with the anus of bilaterian animals (worms, humans, snails, fish etc.). Furthermore, they possess a third tissue layer between the endoderm and ectoderm, another characteristic reminiscent of the Bilateria. However, molecular data has contradicted this view, although only weakly.

Once you've read this, you realise how distinct Golding's writing truly is. Distinctness that might satisfy Carey's theoretical requirements would be unreadably technical – as is the passage above to anyone but a zoologist.

If, like John Carey, you believe that metaphor and simile are unnatural, anti-rational procedures – 'fitting things together that rational thought would keep apart' – and if you therefore believe that metaphor 'is the gateway to the subconscious', you will be predisposed to find metaphor inexplicable and baffling.

Carey is, for instance, baffled by Shylock's lament when he hears that his daughter Jessica has exchanged a ring for a monkey: 'Thou torturest me, Tubal – it was my turquoise, I had it of Leah when I was a bachelor: I would not have given it for a wilderness of monkeys.' Carey thinks 'wilderness of monkeys' a phrase beyond Marlowe – in its indistinctness. There is nothing baffling to me here. His runaway daughter has given away a ring with deep sentimental associations for Shylock in exchange for a brute beast. The power is in the laconic back-story, whose economy is the guarantee of its truth. The wilderness of monkeys is partly a neologism, a new collective noun and completely comprehensible as such: a herd of sheep, a flock of birds, a wilderness of monkeys. And it is partly the idea of a place without a trace of the human, entirely given over to animals, to monkeys. Or, in *Titus Andronicus*, 'a wilderness of tigers': 'Rome is but a wilderness of tigers.' That is what a wilderness is – a place uninhabited by human beings. Carey wonders whether the wilderness is 'trees and grass', whether the monkeys are different kinds of monkeys, whether there are animals other than monkeys. He even wonders if the monkeys have tails or not. He might ask with as much literary purpose if the monkeys are supporters of Manchester United or Glasgow Rangers. All these questions, if asked, if answered, would bury the idea in irrelevant distinctnesses. It is clear enough as it stands.

This is Carey on Tennyson's *Maud*: the hero finds as he walks in the night 'the shining daffodil dead, and Orion low in his grave'. The daffodil, Carey says, comes from nowhere. 'No mention of a daffodil, or even of a garden, in the poem up to this point.' I don't think that a prior mention of daffodils – a plant – would have helped Professor Carey. Wordsworth's host of golden daffodils don't require a garden. They are surely wild. Then Carey wants to know if the daffodil is real or imaginary, because it is shining and dead daffodils are dull. Ergo, a dead shining daffodil is probably imaginary and exists 'only in the mind'. Literalism again making problems for itself. Tennyson only means that the shining, the once shining daffodil, is now dead. Compare Shakespeare on dandelions/youth: 'Golden lads and girls all must / As chimney-sweepers come to dust.' The 'golden lad is dead' doesn't mean that his corpse isn't grey and with sunken eyelids.

Matthew Arnold's 'To a Gipsy Child by the Sea-shore' contains lines that baffle him too:

> Ah! Not the nectarous poppy lovers use,
> Not daily labour's dull, Lethaean spring,
> Oblivion in lost angels can infuse
> Of the soiled glory, and the trailing wing.

If we straighten out the inversion the sense will be easier: neither the drug of love, nor the grind of work, can infuse in lost angels oblivion of the soiled glory and trailing wing. For Carey, this suggests a wounded bird – a red herring gull perhaps – about which he speculates fruitlessly since Arnold is invoking angels. Arnold is saying this: all human beings have a fugitive but ineradicable sense of impaired spirituality, an imperfect spiritual dimension, so that, were we angels, we would have a faint consciousness of glory – but soiled glory – and of wings – but ineffectual wings. The 'haunting indistinctness' Carey locates in these lines is in his reading, not in Arnold's writing. Carey has created it. DIY fog. Home-made Moonshine.

What is really going on here? Think back to Carey's comments on the Housman poem – his objection that 'a cuckoo may be in a dell but it cannot be in dells'. The determination to misread, the predisposition not to make sense, not to make easy sense of the poem, to refuse delivery of its meaning, is the mark of deconstruction. Professor Carey, without advertising it, contrary to all previous critical outings, has become a deconstructionist. Someone has given him a present – a chainsaw, the chainsaw of deconstruction, with its insistence on meaninglessness – and he is applying it vigorously to everything in sight. Everywhere wailing, whining, the gnashing of teeth and the smell of petrol. And of course, maimed poetry, maimed writing, lopped into unreadable fragments.

He quotes from Tennyson's 'The Lotos Eaters': 'like a downward smoke, the slender stream / Along the cliff to fall and pause and fall did seem.' He comments with deconstructionist pedantry: 'the hesitant "fall and pause and fall" slows them up so much they actually stop, and likening them to smoke takes away all their urgency and weight, even while it is supposed to be signifying the perpetual fog of spray caused by the mass of displaced water.' (But Tennyson's lines aren't *supposed* to be signifying a *mass* of displaced water. They are describing something made smaller by distance.)

Carey identifies a 'lie', the contradiction: 'the falls would be noisy, but we hear nothing; Tennyson makes them fall very slowly and gently, as they obviously would not if you were close to them'. All the difficulty here – the wherefore of the spatial illusion, how Tennyson makes the falls so far off – is of Carey's own making. There is no *illusion*, no trick. Tennyson is merely describing how waterfalls look – and do not sound – from a distance. Nothing mysterious about that pause in the falling either: the waterfall disappears from sight. You wonder what he would make of Wordsworth's crossing the Alps in Book VI of *The Prelude*: 'the stationary blasts of waterfalls'. Which is an impossibility and therefore indistinct. Unless you register the precision, the distinctness of Wordsworth's description – that the waterfall, whose constituents are changing every second, *appears* also to be permanently in place.

And what are we to make of Carey's reading of Keats's 'Ode on a Grecian Urn'?

> Who are these coming to the sacrifice?
> To what green altar, O mysterious priest,
> Lead'st thou that heifer lowing at the skies,
> And all her silken flanks with garlands drest?
> What little town by river or sea shore,
> Or mountain-built with peaceful citadel,
> Is emptied of this folk, this pious morn?
> And, little town, thy streets for evermore,
> Will silent be; and not a soul to tell
> Why thou art desolate, can e'er return.

In the ode, apparently, Keats enacts the same process Carey postulates for his reader – the creation of something from nothing, reality from indistinctness. The stanza is, Carey says, 'about trying to make indistinctness distinct, as readers of literature do'. He insists that there is no town, no people, no streets – because these are representations on an urn. Carey: 'But against these peremptory denials Keats's lines build an alternative town, indistinct, imaginary and indestructible.' Whose peremptory denials? Carey's peremptory denials. No one else's. Actually, the stanza works like this: Keats peers curiously at the depicted scene to see what is depicted there – but this immediately confers reality on the people 'coming to the sacrifice', because the sacrifice isn't explained or prepared for.

It is assumed. The altar is green. The heifer is vividly, distinctly present: 'her silken flanks with garlands drest'.

Keats is quite distinct about what he doesn't see on the side of the urn. The undetermined location of the little town – by a river, by the sea, in the mountains – is important to Keats's purpose because he wants to balance the irresistible reality of his creation with a reminder that he is also describing the picture on an urn. He wants to draw attention to the art involved in the distinctness of his evocation. Carey is wrong. The picture isn't indistinct. It is overwhelmingly distinct, with one brief, clear and distinct equivocation to advertise his creative mastery.

There is a contradiction, another hole in Carey's argument here. If Keats is doing what the reader normally does – that is, supplying detail to indistinctness – then the reader's help isn't required. And if it isn't required here, why is it ever required? The artist is the artist – not the reader. Carey's thesis is a variant on Oscar Wilde's not entirely coherent idea of The Critic as Artist – namely, the reader as artist.

Unfortunately, as we have seen, this involves the average reader, the ordinary reader and the ham-fisted reader, as well as the attentive reader.

# Chapter Nine

## Getting it Wrong

As an undergraduate, I was taught by Jonathan Wordsworth, the poet's grand-nephew. One week he set two poems of Donne, 'A Nocturnall upon S. Lucies Day' and 'The Canonization'. Two poems. It was a trap. I should have realised. I read them an hour before the tutorial. I was about to be taught a lesson, a lesson I have never forgotten. The tutorial took the form of an inquisition. Jonathan asked me what everything in each poem meant. For example, what did 'Yea, stones detest and love' mean? I hadn't the faintest idea. Might it mean, Jonathan suggested, in the falsetto comic Cockney voice he reserved for mockery, that lodestones had magnetic properties and therefore like magnets could attract and repel, detest and love?

In the church of Santi Apostoli in Venice, there is a Tullio Lombardo bas-relief bust of a naked man in the right-hand side-altar. It's marble, a panel 51 centimetres high and 40 centimetres wide. Art historians think it is St Sebastian – without any arrows, to be sure, but with a look of mild agony on his face and a pruned tree trunk behind his head, with three oak leaves flourishing from one lopped branch. St Sebastian is usually bound to a tree, hence the association. No one has dissented from this identification. The art historian Debra Pincus notes that 'the eyes [are] opened wide and turned upward but entirely blank', as they sometimes are in sculpture (though not often in

Lombardo, who is something of an eye specialist sculpturally, with some notable innovations).

In fact, this isn't a skewed, slightly fuzzy representation of St Sebastian. It is a brilliant representation of a blind man. The agonised mouth isn't agonised at all. Like the slightly gathered brows, it captures, with complete accuracy, that wariness we sometimes see on blind faces, the anticipation of possible pain rather than pain itself. After all, what is out there, waiting to hurt you, if you are blind?

And the tree trunk, so candidly lopped? An objective correlative of disability, of loss – with the idea of compensation, adaptation, a kind of recovery, possibly the idea of spiritual advantage, of introspection now the natural world has vanished.

(Soon, I daresay, the art historians will be telling us this is a representation of Saul's blindness on the road to Damascus. It isn't. It's about blindness.)

Once we realise what this sculpture means, its brilliance, its virtuosity is transparent. It has been rescued from the labyrinth of explanations – from what Jeremy Noel-Tod calls the 'hermeneutics of endless enquiry'. We see it for what it is. Not as some murky impostor, some art-historical photo-fit, assimilating it to a hundred other 'identical' works of art. It means something very particular, something absolutely specific. If you drink tea thinking it is coffee, the experience is unpleasant.

I repeat, the most important question you can ask of a poem is, What does this poem mean? It is not the only question to ask of a poem, but it is the one without which all other questions are likely to be misdirected.

Many academics prefer not to ask or answer this question. For them it is crude and reductive. If they say what a poem 'means', there is a real risk also that they will get it wrong, demonstrably wrong. If they have been taught English at Cambridge, they will have been trained to maximise the semantic possibilities of any poetic text. Close reading in Cambridge means a multiplicity of local effects – the exercise of critical ingenuity, the identification of ambiguities that make an over-view impossible. It is a given that poetry is inexhaustible, that there are no right answers.

And Oxford? When John Carey became Merton Professor of English at Oxford, his inaugural lecture was called 'The Critic as Vandal: The Heresy of Paraphrase'. In it, he demon-strated, with his customary stringent wit, how inaccurate the paraphrases of many critics had been. Nevertheless, paraphrase is an essential, if necessarily approximate, tool in literary dis-course. Without it, we preserve a kind of purity, but at the cost of not knowing where we stand, roughly speaking.

Many academics (and some poets) prefer to concentrate on local effects – assonance, rhythm, poetic micro-effects. If they do address the question of meaning, something interesting happens – commonly they find current critical preoccupa-tions asserting their presence in the poems. As it might be, the body, the inadequacy of language, political sub-text, political encryption.

And in a way, it is both inevitable and proper to identify these things in poetry and literature. (Every age is different. We all agree that literature in foreign languages should be retrans-lated for every age.) It's proper except when it is improper. (Actually, I don't accept the translation argument. Constance Garnett's translations of Chekhov are better than those of Ronald Hingley for two reasons: one, her literary gifts are greater than his; two, she is Chekhov's contemporary so her register is, more or less, identical to Chekhov. Were he to have written in English, Garnett's English is the kind of English Chekhov would have written.)

When is paraphrase *improper*? When it involves a mis-description of the poem, when the poem is skewed to fit the thesis already mapped out in the critic's mind. It's improper when the reading is like a jigsaw – a jigsaw in which a piece from another jigsaw, the critic's own jigsaw, can be seen bulging from where it has been forced.

For instance, a critic might want to demonstrate what a sexually enlightened New Man he is – sensitive to female delicacy, wary of voyeurism, wary of 'the male gaze', wary of any gesture smacking of patriarchy or exploitation. For instance, Tom Paulin (in *The Secret Life of Poems* and *The Minotaur*) writing about two poems by Emily Dickinson ('He fumbles at your Soul' and 'I never lost as much but twice').

He fumbles at your Soul
As Players at the Keys
Before they drop full Music on –
He stuns you by degrees –

Prepares your brittle Nature
For the Ethereal Blow
By fainter Hammers – further heard –
Then nearer – Then so slow

Your Breath has time to straighten –
Your Brain – to bubble Cool –
Deals – One – imperial – Thunderbolt –
That scalps your naked Soul –

When Winds take Forests in their Paws –
The Universe – is still –

'He', the subject, is Death.

Generally, incorrectly, Dickinson readers have thought the subject to be a preacher – if not a groper and a bodice-ripper with clumsy, ugly fingers, then bent on domineering over susceptible women.

As in 'Because I could not stop for Death', Dickinson's idea is that very few of us die suddenly. We go into a decline. Death is a gradual process – sometimes with remission, but ending in a climax. Hence the extended pianism metaphor, and its references to diminuendo and forte.

Let me add a few words of extra explanation. 'Your Breath has time to straighten': 'straighten' meaning become regular, steady, to stop being uneven. 'Your Brain – to bubble Cool': after fever, say, or a temperature, you stabilise. The image is of cold spring-water bubbling away. Dying isn't always a steady, uniform progress down to the grave. There are fluctuations in the condition of the dying person. Overall, however, the direction is irreversible. An analogy: if you eat an *Amanita virosa*, the 'avenging angel' mushroom, you will die. The symptoms of recovery on the third day, the mushroom books tell us, are *always* illusory.

'Deals' isn't properly linked syntactically: it comes suddenly, without syntactic preparation, like death itself. The image of scalping is an image of separation, of soul from the body.

What do the last two lines mean and how do they relate to the rest of the poem? 'When Winds take Forests in their Paws – / The Universe – is still –' is only a partial change in direction because it is still an image of destructive power. Either the paws tear apart the forests, or they toy with forests. Either way, the wind's power is granted, and the plural, 'forests', is an important indicator.

These two final lines may mean that even a cataclysmic

event is as nothing in terms of the universe. It remains undisturbed, unaffected. In terms of the individual death, one person's demise is as nothing in the larger scheme of things.

Or the lines might conceivably mean that the universe is watching raptly, on hold, while the individual death takes place. My preference is for the former reading. That the destruction of forests is as nothing seen against the universe – and therefore the individual death is an intense but eminently local event.

Where did the completely irrelevant idea of the preacher come from? Answer: from the mention of 'soul' in the first line. But of course, in death the soul leaves the body. Read like this, the poem is simple. And the simplicity, the fit of this solution to the words on the page, is how we know the reading is right. The principle of Occam's razor is sound. William of Occam believed that, if there were two possible interpretations of a phenomenon, we should prefer the simplest.

This is Tom Paulin, vaunting his feminist credentials, and turning Dickinson's poem into a peevish, spinsterish complaint about men and their ways: 'she is suspicious of a masculine use of sexual attraction and of female response to it' [those benighted women *responding* to sexual interest]; 'in her mind's eye she can see a man's hand trying to undo a woman's bodice. The action is clumsy, ugly, dominant, intrusive.' It is also entirely imagined by Tom Paulin: there is no hand in the poem, no bodice, and the assumption that when men undo women's bodices this is always clumsy and undesired goes against the grain of many women's experiences. In Maupassant's *Bel Ami*, Georges Duroy's fingers are rather nimble and practised. But it would never do for Paulin to grant maleness delicacy of touch, or to admit that women might want to have their bodices undone. There is an unspoken assumption here with the force of a law. It is this. Men are gross.

In order to occupy this moral high ground, from where he can deplore male moral shortcomings, Paulin has to massage the meaning of Dickinson's poem. The male figure in 'He fumbles at your Soul' is, Paulin argues, a pianist, a preacher giving a sermon, leading the woman into an abattoir, the blacksmith's forge or church to be married. The wedding is not a happy event but 'the heavenly hammer blow that is marriage in a church to a man in a ceremony presided over by a male priest'.

In case you were wondering, this marriage ceremony takes place only in Tom Paulin's head, not in Emily Dickinson's poem.

The male figure contains multitudes, according to Paulin. His multiple identity encompasses pianist, preacher, blacksmith, slaughter-house employee, burglar and bridegroom. All these are dubious readings, but 'burglar' is without a shred of justification.

*I promise you I am not making this up.*

Paulin continues: 'Here the free female spirit struggles with a murderous patriarch.' At this juncture, Paulin refers to the Dickinson poem via the prism of *Washington Square* and Austin Sloper. His reading of the novel is equally incompetent. The 'murderous patriarch' is specifically ruled out by Henry James's text, only to be ruled in by Paulin, even as he quotes the text: 'There was a kind of still intensity about her father which made him dangerous, *but Catherine hardly went so far as to say to herself* [my italics] that it might be part of his plan to fasten his hand – the neat, fine, supple hand of a distinguished physician – in her throat.' James's point is that the Alpine setting suggests the perfect setting for the melodramatic events of cheap fiction. The reality, however, is different.

If Tom Paulin can't read prose, it doesn't bode well for poetry. Sure enough, we read about the 'close assonance in "full Music"' – we are told that this assonance 'is attractive – those *oo* sounds'. And this attractiveness is deceptive, a siren song. Actually, the attractiveness *is* deceptive – mainly because the assonance, those *oo* sounds, are a figment of Tom Paulin's erratic, unreliable ear – sadly for a critic who sets so much store by his sensitivity to aural effects. The 'u' in 'full' is different from the 'u' in 'music'. Only one 'u' sound is an *oo* sound and that is the 'u' in 'music'. The 'u' in 'full' is more like 'uh'. Of course, an Ulsterman might conceivably pronounce 'full' with an 'oo' sound, were he Ian Paisley. But Emily Dickinson wasn't an Ulsterman.

Paulin's analysis of sound effects in Derek Mahon's 'A Disused Shed in Co. Wexford' is equally erratic: '"shed" assonating with "asphodels"'. Shed doesn't assonate with asphodels. 'And as the shed is burnt-out, we see "ash" in "asphodels", and associate it with the death camps.' The shed isn't burnt-out. The hotel, in whose grounds the shed is, is burnt-out. (You begin to see the usefulness of paraphrase. Without it, we wouldn't know how wrong Paulin's readings were.)

This is Paulin's scanning of Mahon's first line: 'Even now there are places where a thought might grow –'. It is, he maintains, 'a classical alexandrine, a line of six mainly iambic feet, with the caesura after "places" and the reversed iambic foot "where a".' There is no caesura after 'places'. '-es where a thought may grow' is a regular iambic trimeter. 'Where a' is not a reversed foot. 'Even now' is an anapaest. So is 'there are place'. So, two anapaests and an iambic trimeter.

A digression. No poet is born with a perfect ear. The ear of the poet has to be trained. Practice, and more practice, makes almost perfect. Tennyson was proud of his ear. He quoted the opening line of Pope's *The Rape of the Lock* in a phonetic rendering ('What dire offence from amruz causiz springz...') and declared he would rather be dead than write such a line. It is said that Tennyson knew the quantity of every word in the English language – except for 'scissors'. This puzzles me, because 'scissors' is a natural trochee. How come Tennyson couldn't settle the quantity? I once discussed this with the poet Edward Lucie-Smith, who suggested the following resolution: that, although 'scissors' *is* a trochee, with the stress on the first syllable, the first vowel 'sciss' is closed, whereas the second 'ors' is open. Tennyson did have a remarkable ear. He was right to be vain about it. His blank verse is exceptionally varied. His local effects can be beautiful and intricate. (See my examples in Chapter Five on the lyric.) This doesn't make *The Idylls of the King* or long passages of *The Princess* more than competent at best and tedious at worst. Sometimes it's difficult not to see Tennyson's ear as comparable to a tennis player's overdeveloped arm, or a porn star's penis – useful, striking, but manifestly insufficient on its own.

Digression over. More worrying than these aural bodges and local mistakes is the way Tom Paulin gets the overall meaning, the authorial intention, of both Dickinson poems completely wrong. I turn now to Dickinson's 'I never lost as much but twice'.

> I never lost as much but twice,
> And that was in the sod.
> Twice have I stood a beggar
> Before the door of God!
>
> Angels – twice descending
> Reimbursed my store –
> Burglar! Banker – Father!
> I am poor once more!

'I never lost as much but twice' isn't a love lyric. It isn't spoken by Emily Dickinson. It is voiced for a bereaved mother and addressed to God, who has taken her children away, given her replacements, and taken those away too. Dickinson makes a bold equation of God (who giveth and taketh away) with the banker and the burglar, the banker who giveth and the burglar who taketh away.

Tom Paulin's 'reading' of this simple poem – 'another of her love lyrics' – is a perverse miracle of misprision. He argues in *The Minotaur* that 'I never lost as much but twice' is addressed to a lover by Emily Dickinson and that she is protesting 'against the dominant masculine values of nineteenth-century American culture'.

Paul Muldoon's 'Quoof' is a genuinely difficult poem. Here are three critics – Tim Kendall, Clair Wills and (not sorry about this) Tom Paulin again – all getting it wrong.

Clair Wills, in her introduction to *Reading Paul Muldoon*, writes: 'Muldoon's poetry continually struggles with the desire to transform experience into an aesthetic artefact, while recognising the impossibility of fully grasping it.' Behind this idea, that art will always fail to equal experience, is a theoretical commonplace – that the signifier is fatally adrift from the signified, so there will always be a gap between art and reality since it is a condition of language. And so it proves. I apologise in advance for her painful exposition:

> The shocking and disturbing character of the language of *Quoof* is clearly in part an exploration of the limits of the poetic, and indeed the limits of language in general. For one of the central preoccupations of *Quoof* is the problem of communicating what is most intimate, even repulsive. Muldoon wonders how one can transform the private, per-

sonal world (at the extreme, the body) [that fashionable theoretical topos] into something with public meaning. Language is normally taken to be the way in which the raw contingency of our existence (of which the body and its processes are perhaps the most extreme examples) is transmuted into something with publicly acknowledged significance. But the paradox is that the closer language gets to the intimate core of the self, the less it is able to communicate at all. Thus language becomes both the means of escape and a form of containment. The title poem, another sonnet, and perhaps the most enigmatic poem in the book is also built around ideas of containment and escape. It questions whether it is ever possible to communicate the familial and personal... the whole person is encased in a private language.

The body – that fashionable theoretical topos. Remember? A few pages back? 'If they [academics] do address the question of meaning, something interesting happens – commonly they find current critical preoccupations asserting their presence in the poems. As it might be, *the body, the inadequacy of language*, political sub-text, political encryption.' [my italics]

Here's the title poem 'Quoof', the Muldoon family name for a hot water bottle:

> How often have I carried our family word
> for the hot water bottle
> to a strange bed,
> as my father would juggle a red-hot half-brick
> in an old sock
> to his childhood settle.
> I have taken it into so many lovely heads

or laid it between us like a sword.

An hotel room in New York City
with a girl who spoke hardly any English,
my hand on her breast
like the smouldering one-off spoor of the yeti
or some other shy beast
that has yet to enter the language.

Wills's interpretation concludes by denying its own conviction, its definitiveness as a reading, by asserting its own arbitrariness: 'the poem doesn't allow for a definitive interpretation'. Typically, she resists the imperative to assign a meaning. *In case she is wrong.* She says there is no obvious relationship between the octet and the sestet. Its continuity, she maintains, is held together by the rhyme scheme. 'The reader has to track the poet through this scenery like the unknown yeti. [And here the Saussurean gap between signifier and signified is explicitly and predictably invoked] Characteristically in this poem we see not the beast, but the sign of the beast, and the fact that the spoor is smouldering suggests that we have just missed it. [Or come extremely close to seeing it: a contradictory case Wills would not want to consider.] This is an emblem for the poem's own evasiveness, for a more elusive poem would be hard to imagine.' So, in summary: we don't know what the poem means and that is what the poem means.

That said – safely, conclusively inconclusive – Wills makes several provisional observations. Father is provincial. Son is cosmopolitan. The sexual body replaces the hot water bottle as a source of warmth and comfort. The word 'quoof' asserts the continuity between father and son. The son is unable to break free from family tradition. [There is *no* indication he *wants* to.]

She notes, despite his Irishness, Muldoon's exaggerated command of English: 'An hotel.' She wonders whether he isn't trying to slough off 'the burdens of the tribe' ('quoof' being a kind of shibboleth). I can tell her that 'an hotel' was my suggestion as Muldoon's editor. It is grammatically correct. The trouble with Wills's comments is that they are discrete, discontinuous, imposed on the poem.

In one case, the comment is demonstrably wrong. Viz: 'his hand is being compared to the print of an animal.' Tom Paulin thinks that 'spoor' is a pile of shit rather than a print, but he agrees that it is Muldoon's hand which is being compared to the spoor of the yeti. Wrongly. In both cases. It is the woman's breast which is like 'the smouldering one-off spoor of the yeti'. The hunter, the tracker, puts his hand on the spoor, the droppings, to judge their heat, to find out how recent the droppings are. So the breast is the spoor.

This is Tim Kendall on 'Quoof'. He disagrees with Clair Wills. 'The poem opens with what sounds like a question, or even a rhetorical brag about sexual adventure.' Like Wills, Kendall thinks the poem is a contrast, an extreme contrast, between those two old chestnuts innocence and experience, childhood innocence and cosmopolitan experience. Kendall's reading is that the word 'quoof' is a shibboleth which therefore can exclude or include. 'The word selects sexual partners willing to enter the poet's inner world, while barring those – like the girl who speaks "hardly any English" – who will not or cannot.' This is exactly wrong.

For Paulin, the poem is in dialogue with Heaney's 'Broagh'. The red-hot brick in its sock suggests 'sex and danger' – and a condom – as well as bricks thrown in riots during the Troubles. 'Quoof' carries suggestions of 'quim' and 'loofah'. It is, therefore, a jokey word. Loofah! I am not joking. By saying he has laid it like a sword between himself and women – according to Paulin – it signifies 'marital division and refusal of sex'. There is no indication whatsoever that marital discord is an issue. The speaker is manifestly behaving like a bachelor. As for the girl in the hotel room in New York City, Paulin sees the speaker as 'an English-speaking imperial male as he lays his hand on the breast of the unnamed girl who speaks hardly any English'.

It is difficult to say what Paulin thinks the poem is actually about. Via Patrick Kavanagh's 'Kerr's Ass', he concludes that 'both poems are about emigration, language, identity'. Kavanagh's poem mentions Ealing Broadway, London Town. Paulin thinks this alludes to Broadway in New York, 'an image of fame and artistic success'. And concludes that 'Quoof' – which doesn't mention Broadway either in London or New York – is therefore about the cost of success in America.

What does the poem actually mean? It is a poem about Muldoon losing his virginity to a prostitute in New York City – after the usual series of non-consummated embarrassing sexual encounters that commonly precede the first time. In these encounters the sexual impulse morphs into warmth, comfort, hot water bottles and the family word for them. The cosiness of the word is prophylactic: 'laid it between us like a sword.' All the intercourse is mental rather than corporeal: 'I have taken it into so many lovely heads.' The key here is Muldoon's father juggling the hot brick – which is a figure of speech for embarrassment. With the girl 'who spoke hardly any English', Muldoon can't talk his way out of it.

The yeti represents the unknown – in this case, sexual experience, once Muldoon gets over his shyness. The connection between the octet and the sestet is this: in the octet a familiar family word is strange; in the sestet, a strange, unknown thing is about to become familiar. The sonnet observes the traditional *versus* of the sonnet. Shyness is common to both the octet and the sestet – it is disabling and it is overcome. The boastfulness that Kendall identifies in the octet is actually its opposite.

Yeats's 'Byzantium' has been misread by so many critics that it would be impossible – as well as worthless – to summarise them. But it is possible to say that the shared mistake of these misreadings, or non-readings, is the reliance on background knowledge instead of close reading. In the *Norton Anthology of Poetry*, the notes refer us to *Apotheosis and After-Life* (1915) by Mrs Arthur Strong, 'a book on Roman sculpture that Yeats is believed to have known'. Generally cited, too, are quotations from *A Vision* or other bits of Yeats's inspissated prose. My copy of Yeats has quotations from *A Vision* and Yeats's Diary pencilled in the margin. Neither helps. A key rule of thumb: resist all readings that rely on concurrent citation either of poems by the same author, or (in the case of Tom Paulin) of poems by other authors – as if multiplication of the problem will solve the problem.

The opening stanza sets the scene in Byzantium and sets up the crucial contrast between the completeness of art – here a dome – and fragmentary human nature, the unpurged, the impure, the tarts, the pissed soldiers.

Stanza two describes Yeats's vision of the superhuman. Its constituent identity is between ghost (or shade) and man. It has a mouth that has no moisture and no breath. Here there is a syntactical ambiguity. Either the superhuman can summon 'breathless mouths' – i.e. more like itself. Or, more likely, 'breathless mouths' – meaning mouths that are holding their breath – can summon this superhuman whose mouth does not breathe. 'I call it death-in-life and life-in-death': so in some sense, it transcends mortality.

Stanza three invokes a golden bird, an artefact, as the super-human, in precisely the same way, via *qualification*: 'shade more than man, more image than a shade'. The bird is 'Miracle, bird or golden handiwork, / More miracle than bird or handiwork'. So the superhuman and the bird are aligned by their shared definitional epitomes. And they also return us to the starlit dome of stanza one: the golden bird scorns 'in glory of change-less metal' 'all complexities of mire or blood' – the human, the bodily, the decaying, the mortal.

Stanza four evokes the purgative fire which will purify the 'unpurged images of day' of stanza one. 'Blood-begotten spir-its' come here and 'leave' their human complexities behind, their 'fury' at mortality.

Stanza five is the stumper. What is going on here?

> Astraddle on the dolphin's mire and blood,
> Spirit after spirit! The smithies break the flood,
> The golden smithies of the Emperor!
> Marbles of the dancing floor
> Break bitter furies of complexity,
> Those images that yet
> Fresh images beget,
> That dolphin-torn, that gong-tormented sea.

Our difficulty is partly the result of Yeats's expository incom-petence, his wayward way with words. 'Gong-tormented' returns us to the 'great cathedral gong' of the opening stanza. Obviously, in general terms, Yeats is describing the vision of the dead being transported to the underworld on the backs of dol-phins – dolphins because they are immersed in the sea and out of the sea, both in the element and out of the element.

The smithies are the problem, 'the golden smithies of the

Emperor'. They are not 'golden' at all. They are the gold-smiths who fashion the golden bird of stanza three. The other wholly misleading word is the verb 'break' which sug-gests that these smithies use their hammers to smash up the 'flood' – the sea. More, the two lines – 'Marbles of the dancing floor / Break bitter furies of complexity' – sound as if the marble dancing floor breaks up and turns into bitter furies of complexity. Whatever that might mean. But Yeats means something else. In fact, Yeats intends to repeat the statement of the first stanza where the starlit dome 'disdains' 'all that man is'. Here the verb 'break' doesn't mean 'smash' – it means 'opposes', 'destroys' or 'defeats'. (Compare the idea of break-ing the flow of someone's thought.) The golden handiwork of the smithies, that golden bird on a golden bough, breaks or *defeats* the flood. They have achieved ascendancy over human flux through artistic permanence. And the marble dancing floor ('Dying into a dance') *defeats* 'bitter furies of complexity'.

However, Yeats concludes that the battle between flux and permanence, between mortality and unchanging artefact, between the merely human and the superhuman, rages forever because 'those images' beget 'fresh images'.

I am aware – how could I not be? – that my interpretation's coherence rests on the dubious premise that Yeats's use of lan-guage is inexact, or isn't quite exact enough. To understand poetry, the first rule is careful attention to the precise words actually used. In my defence, I can point to the unsuccessful and incoherent plethora of readings of 'Byzantium' – pages of nonsense that leave the poetry nonsense. And I would say that I am reading carefully. My sense of Yeats's verb 'breaks' is available. It just isn't the obvious first choice. My reading of 'Byzantium' abides by two cardinal rules: that the first task we require of poetry is to *mean* something. Second, when we read, we eliminate unhelpful connotations of words and look for the relevant meaning – the one which unlocks the sense of the poem. Deconstruction is no way to read poetry.

# Coda

---

## *Goe Littel Boke*

Poetry puts the world in italics.

It adds emphasis. Three examples: examples that are related to the surreal, which have a flavour of the surreal, without being surreal. These examples of reality tweaked come from Tennessee Williams. They are the titles of plays. *A Streetcar Named Desire. The Glass Menagerie. Sweet Bird of Youth.* Anyone who has read or seen *The Glass Menagerie* will know that Williams had a weakness for poetry restricted to high lyricism, to the singing line. (Which he handed on to Arthur Miller, who mostly restricted it to the stage directions.) These three titles have lost their poetry by now, just as street names escape their origins: Alma Place refers no longer to the battle of Alma in the Crimean War. Palmerston Road is a street by now rather than a tribute to a statesman. Similarly, Tennessee Williams's titles denote the plays. Their poetry, their strangeness, no longer strikes us – the combination of streetcar and desire, of menagerie and glass. Whereas William Burroughs's surreal title *The Naked Lunch* is still bizarre.

In Bede's *Ecclesiastical History of the English People* there is an image of the soul as a bird in flight through a great hall. It is cognate with Williams's sweet bird of youth, waiting to migrate, waiting to fly away. The poetry is there still – if you pay attention. And poetry is there to make you pay attention

– to underline the obvious, which has become unobvious, unseen, invisible because we are overfamiliar with it. Poetry is a snag, an obstacle to smoothness. It stops us in our tracks. *A Streetcar Named Desire*. What does it mean? It is as unlikely as surrealism, but it makes sense. It says something about love and its transfigurative power, the way desire can lend charisma to the commonplace. So it is about Stella's love for her Pollack, Stanley Kowalski. And it is about Blanche's doomed desire to beautify her past, to gift it a bogus poetry.

Poetry is a lie that serves the truth.

Poetry is a disguise that reveals.

I began this little book by looking at the word 'poetry' as it appeared in fiction. I think that these unconsidered, unworried, inadvertent references uncover interesting assumptions about the way we think about poetry, about what we think poetry is, when we're not trying to explain it or define it. So I'll end in the same way.

In J. D. Salinger's *Raise High the Roof Beam, Carpenters*, Buddy Glass is stuck in a cab with other wedding guests. The atmosphere is tense because the bridegroom, Seymour Glass, has apparently jilted his bride-to-be. The occupants of the cab include an uncle of the bride's father, a deaf-mute so small that his top hat doesn't reach the roof of the cab and his feet don't touch the floor. He holds in his fingers an unlit cigar. Buddy writes an invitation to the deaf-mute inviting him to a cold drink in Schrafft's.

In answer, the old man writes one word in pencil on the pad – *delighted*. Which Buddy recognises as a poem by a great writer. Salinger's perfect paragraph uses 128 words to tell us this: it is the writerly equivalent of a tea ceremony – a ritual meticulously notated, every movement, every micro-adjustment, every note, every nuance registered. The paragraph does nothing remarkable yet mimics inspiration – the long unbroken intake of breath. A poem!

I know this is hyperbole. I know, too, that readers unsympathetic to Salinger are likely to see it invidiously as situated somewhere between sentimental and cute. But the sound assumption behind it is this: poetry means minimal words for maximum impact. Here, one word, one allegedly saturated word. Delighted.

In 1984, I was invited by an advertising agency, Davidson Pearce, to write a poem to launch a new fragrance by Chesbrough-Ponds, the manufacturers of Vaseline. First of all, I met the secretary to the assistant to the creative director. She told me that Alexis, as it was called, didn't smell very nice. Then I was swept off by the assistant and silently conducted into the presence of the creative director. He briefed me about the profile of the new product. It would be a very upmarket fragrance, bought by classy women who wore Burberry and took their holidays not abroad but in Devon. (Definitely not the expensive hooker look of Versace, then.) And that, he said, is why we want to hire you – because poetry is the very opposite of advertising.

No, I said, you're wrong: advertising and poetry are exactly the same. Minimum words, maximum impact. The difference is that poets do it better. We're classier. Some of us are classic.

However, the economy of the poem is, as it were, single crop. Put it another way, the difference between a poem and a novel is the difference between a pill and a surgical procedure taking several hours. It's easy to forget you've taken a pill, so poetry has to make itself memorable. It has to hold you for long enough to become memorable.

Back to *Raise High the Roof Beam, Carpenters*. In the same story, Seymour Glass, the recalcitrant groom, meditates in his diary on Tao and the idea of accepting imperfection and weakness. The Tao philosophy, he finds, is irreconcilable with poetry. Why? Tao is the acceptance of imperfection. To follow Tao means giving up poetry. Therefore, poetry is perfection, the opposite of imperfection. And it seems to be aesthetic, at odds with the ethical imperative of the Tao.

As the reader already knows by now, I am impatient with those big balsa-wood claims poets often make for poetry, but there is something sound here, too. Poetry uses very few words. It arranges them artfully – so they *tell*, so they *toll*, so they *travel*. And then it troubles to hide the art, or if not hide it exactly, tries to make it seem natural. Eliot says of verse drama that, although no one in life speaks in verse, successful verse drama depends on the audience thinking that *if* people did speak in verse, *this* is how they might speak. Elizabeth Bishop says: 'Writing poetry is an unnatural act. It takes great skill to make it seem natural.' Her figure for this is her maternal grandmother's glass eye: 'The situation of my grandmother strikes me as rather like the situation of the poet: the difficulty of combining the real with the decidedly un-real; the natural with the unnatural; the curious effect a poem produces of being as normal as *sight* and yet as synthetic, as artificial, as a *glass eye.*'

I think poetry uses language in a not quite ordinary way. Poetry teaches the language to sing. When we sing, the sounds vibrate for longer. We are aware of the sounds. We *make* the sounds. You can't sing without knowing it. Or sing without knowing that singing isn't quite natural. (And we all know what a certain artificial kind of singing sounds like. It sounds like bad poetry. It sits uncomfortably in the ear. And you can see the tendons in its neck. Think Bianca Castafiore in the Tintin books.)

Suzanne Farrell, George Balanchine's last love and muse, was five feet six and a half inches tall. On point, she was six feet one. A good image for the way poetry uses language, the way poetic language is *heightened* language. But always remember how natural Suzanne Farrell seemed on stage, how fluently and how expressively she moved, with not a gesture wasted.

One last thing implicit in the Salinger: Seymour Glass tells his little sister Franny the Tao parable of the horse. The great Tao sage mistakes the gender of the horse and the colour of the horse, but picks out the best horse. The incidentals are less important than the fundamental perfection. I choose to interpret this as follows: the poet may be wrong, as Ezra Pound was wrong about many things, but Pound had an incomparable ear.

On the other hand, I could also interpret the parable to mean that the poet, unlike the philosopher, must get all the details right, the gender, the exact colour, because for the poet these are more important than choosing the right horse. Wisdom is not a requirement for the poet. The ear and the eye are.

Let's look again at Forster's *Howards End*: 'But the poetry of that kiss…' Meaning what exactly? Meaning a transcendence of empirical truth. Helen Schlegel and Paul Wilcox are, for a moment, relieved of the conditions of the purely pragmatic. Meaning that poetry is granted entry, now and then, into the realm of the hypothetical. Meaning that the prosaic can be elevated, transfigured. Or tweaked.

You can say the nursery curtains were striped orange and yellow. Or you can say Orange and lemons sang the jolly striped curtains. You can say a ladder was leaning against a wall. Or you can say a ladder was climbing up the wall. You can say a dumped bedstead was left out in the street. Or you can say a bedstead was sleeping rough. You can say he bought a packet of white sliced bread. Or you can say he bought an accordion of Mother's Pride.

It's a tweak. It's spin. It's paying attention. It's taking nothing for granted. And it isn't the sole prerogative of poetry.

Joyce is a great poet in *Ulysses*. 'Buck Mulligan slit a steaming scone in two and plastered butter across its smoking pith.'

Nabokov is another poet: 'Lolita, light of my life, fire of my loins. My sin, my soul. Lo-lee-ta-: the tip of the tongue taking a trip of three steps down the palate to tap, at three on the teeth. Lo. Lee. Ta.'

You can say that racing cyclists lean forward. Or you can say, as Nabokov does, that the cyclists raced in italics.

Poetry is the addition of italics.

You can say it was twilight. Or you can say, in the French idiom, 'le temps entre le loup et le chien'. You can say, like Alice Oswald, 'A Greyhound in the Evening after a Long Day of Rain' (her title). Or you can say, as she does: 'But what I want to know is / whose is the great grey wicker-limber hound, / like a stepping on coal, going softly away...'

What is happening here is *disguise that reveals*, an occlusion to enhance focus, a beautiful lie that serves the truth. Telling the truth, but telling it slant, as Emily Dickinson advised. Like the glass eye, sometimes improbably angled, of Elizabeth Bishop's grandmother.

In March 2012, I was in New York to see the American production of my daughter's play, *Tribes*. One midday, we were standing outside Grand Central Station, waiting for a friend, before going in to have lunch at the Oyster Bar. My wife pointed something out to me. In the sidewalk, there was a city tree, leafless, an oversized twig. Almost invisible in its atrophied branches was a grimy blue-tit singing inaudibly against the uproar, the outrage of the traffic. If you watched it for long enough, you began to hear something.

These things are an allegory. I am proud to have a trained

ear, an unnecessary feel for cadence, to be a practitioner of an inescapably minority art – but a great art, however misunderstood and unregarded it is in the cacophony of competing ambient, unceasing, undifferentiated noise.

# Appendix: Poems

'A Whole School of Bourgeois Primitives' by Christopher Reid
'A Martian Sends a Postcard Home' by Craig Raine
'Lines for Translation into Any Language' by James Fenton
'[Diogenes]' by Paul Muldoon
'Stuffed' by Carol Ann Duffy
'Ariel' by Sylvia Plath
'A Disused Shed in Co. Wexford' by Derek Mahon
'Goe Lovely Rose' by Edmund Waller
'The Relique' by John Donne
'Old Man' by Edward Thomas
'In Mourning Wise Since Daily I Increase' by Thomas Wyatt
'A Toccata of Galuppi's' by Robert Browning
'Ode on a Grecian Urn' by John Keats
'Polonius' by Miroslav Holub
'Very Simply Topping Up the Brake Fluid' by Simon Armitage
'Never Mind the Quality:' by Simon Armitage
'Cows' by Paul Muldoon

## A Whole School of Bourgeois Primitives

### CHRISTOPHER REID

Our lawn in stripes, the cat's pyjamas,
rain on a sultry afternoon

and the drenching, mnemonic smell this brings us
surging out of the heart of the garden:

these are the sacraments and luxuries
we could not do without.

Welcome to our peaceable kingdom,
where baby lies down with the tiger rug

and bumblebees roll over like puppies
inside foxglove bells...

Here is a sofa, hung by chains
from a gaudy awning.

Two puddles take the sun
in ribbon-patterned canvas chairs.

Our television buzzes like a fancy tie,
before the picture appears –

and jockeys in Art Deco caps and blouses
caress their anxious horses,

looking as smart as the jacks on playing-cards
and as clever as circus monkeys.

Douanier Rousseau had no need to travel
to paint the jungles of his paradise.

One of his tigers, frightened by a thunder-storm,
waves a tail like a loose dressing-gown cord:

it does not seem to match the coat quite,
but is ringed and might prove dangerous.


## A Martian Sends a Postcard Home

CRAIG RAINE

Caxtons are mechanical birds with many wings
and some are treasured for their markings –

they cause the eyes to melt
or the body to shriek without pain.

I have never seen one fly, but
sometimes they perch on the hand.

Mist is when the sky is tired of flight
and rests its soft machine on ground:

then the world is dim and bookish
like engravings under tissue paper.

Rain is when the earth is television.
It has the property of making colours darker.

Model T is a room with the lock inside –
a key is turned to free the world

for movement, so quick there is a film
to watch for anything missed.

But time is tied to the wrist
or kept in a box, ticking with impatience.

In homes, a haunted apparatus sleeps,
that snores when you pick it up.

If the ghost cries, they carry it
to their lips and soothe it to sleep

with sounds. And yet, they wake it up
deliberately, by tickling with a finger.

Only the young are allowed to suffer
openly. Adults go to a punishment room

with water but nothing to eat.
They lock the door and suffer the noises

alone. No one is exempt
and everyone's pain has a different smell.

At night, when all the colours die,
they hide in pairs

and read about themselves –
in colour, with their eyelids shut.

## Lines for Translation into Any Language

JAMES FENTON

1. I saw that the shanty town had grown over the graves
and that the crowd lived among the memorials.

2. It was never very cold – a parachute slung between an
angel and an urn afforded shelter for the newcomers.

3. Wooden beds were essential.

4. These people kept their supplies of gasoline in litre
bottles, which their children sold at the cemetery gates.

5. That night the city was attacked with rockets.

6. The fire brigade bided its time.

7. The people dug for money beneath their beds, to pay the
firemen.

8. The shanty town was destroyed, the cemetery restored.

9. Seeing a plane shot down, not far from the airport, many
of the foreign community took fright.

10. The next day, they joined the queues at the gymnasium,
asking to leave.

11. When the victorious army arrived, they were welcomed by the fire brigade.

12. This was the only spontaneous demonstration in their favour.

13. Other spontaneous demonstrations in their favour were organised by the victors.


## [Diogenes]

### PAUL MULDOON

When Sara stretches into the dark
of the meal-ark

her hand is taken by a hand.
——

A tongue-in-cheek snail goes meticulously
across a mattock's

blade-end.
——

As Southey squats in the claw-foot tub,
oblivious of the shadow-rub

of horses against his tent.

## Stuffed

CAROL ANN DUFFY

I put two yellow peepers in an owl.
Wow. I fix the grin of Crocodile.
Spiv. I sew the slither of an eel.

I jerk, kick-start, the back hooves of a mule.
Wild. I hold a red rag to a bull.
Mad. I spread the feathers of a gull.

I screw a tight snarl to a weasel.
Fierce. I stitch the flippers on a seal.
Splayed. I pierce the heartbeat of a quail.

I like her to be naked and to kneel.
Tame. My motionless, my living doll.
Mute. And afterwards I like her not to tell.


## Ariel

SYLVIA PLATH

Stasis in darkness.
Then the substanceless blue
Pour of tor and distances.

God's lioness,
How one we grow,
Pivot of heels and knees!—The furrow

Splits and passes, sister to
The brown arc
Of the neck I cannot catch,

Nigger-eye
Berries cast dark
Hooks—

Black sweet blood mouthfuls,
Shadows.
Something else

Hauls me through air—
Thighs, hair;
Flakes from my heels.

White
Godiva, I unpeel—
Dead hands, dead stringencies.

And now I
Foam to wheat, a glitter of seas.
The child's cry

Melts in the wall.
And I
Am the arrow,

The dew that flies
Suicidal, at one with the drive
Into the red

Eye, the cauldron of morning.

# A Disused Shed in Co. Wexford

## Derek Mahon

*Let them not forget us, the weak souls among the asphodels. – Seferis,*
*Mythistorema, tr. Keeley and Sherrard*

(for J. G. Farrell)

Even now there are places where a thought might grow —
Peruvian mines, worked out and abandoned
To a slow clock of condensation,
An echo trapped for ever, and a flutter
Of wildflowers in the lift-shaft,
Indian compounds where the wind dances
And a door bangs with diminished confidence,
Lime crevices behind rippling rain-barrels,
Dog corners for bone burials;
And in a disused shed in Co. Wexford,

Deep in the grounds of a burnt-out hotel,
Among the bathtubs and the washbasins
A thousand mushrooms crowd to a keyhole.
This is the one star in their firmament
Or frames a star within a star.
What should they do there but desire?
So many days beyond the rhododendrons
With the world waltzing in its bowl of cloud,
They have learnt patience and silence
Listening to the rooks querulous in the high wood.

They have been waiting for us in a foetor
Of vegetable sweat since civil war days,
Since the gravel-crunching, interminable departure
of the expropriated mycologist.
He never came back, and light since then
Is a keyhole rusting gently after rain.
Spiders have spun, flies dusted to mildew
And once a day, perhaps, they have heard something —
A trickle of masonry, a shout from the blue
Or a lorry changing gear at the end of the lane.

There have been deaths, the pale flesh flaking
Into the earth that nourished it;
And nightmares, born of these and the grim
Dominion of stale air and rank moisture.
Those nearest the door grow strong —
'Elbow room! Elbow room!'
The rest, dim in a twilight of crumbling
Utensils and broken flower-pots, groaning
For their deliverance, have been so long
Expectant that there is left only the posture.

A half century, without visitors, in the dark —

Poor preparation for the cracking lock
And creak of hinges. Magi, moonmen,
Powdery prisoners of the old regime,
Web-throated, stalked like triffids, racked by drought
And insomnia, only the ghost of a scream
At the flash-bulb firing squad we wake them with
Shows there is life yet in their feverish forms.
Grown beyond nature now, soft food for worms,

They lift frail heads in gravity and good faith.

They are begging us, you see, in their wordless way,
To do something, to speak on their behalf
Or at least not to close the door again.
Lost people of Treblinka and Pompeii!
'Save us, save us,' they seem to say,
'Let the god not abandon us
Who have come so far in darkness and in pain.
We too had our lives to live.
You with your light meter and relaxed itinerary,
Let not our naive labours have been in vain!'

## Goe Lovely Rose

EDMUND WALLER

Goe, lovely Rose—
   Tell her that wastes her time and me,
   That now she knows,
When I resemble her to thee,
How sweet and fair she seems to be.

   Tell her that's young,
And shuns to have her graces spied,
   That hadst thou sprung
In deserts where no men abide,
Thou must have uncommended died.

   Small is the worth
Of beauty from the light retired:

Bid her come forth,
Suffer herself to be desired,
And not blush so to be admired.

Then die—that she
The common fate of all things rare
    May read in thee;
How small a part of time they share
That are so wondrous sweet and fair!


## The Relique

JOHN DONNE

When my grave is broke up againe
Some second guest to entertaine,
    (For graves have learn'd that woman-head,
    To be to more than one a Bed)
        And he that digs it, spies
A bracelet of bright haire about the bone,
        Will he not let'us alone,
And thinke that there a loving couple lies,
Who thought that this device might be some way
To make their soules, at the last busie day,
Meet at this grave, and make a little stay?

If this fall in a time, or land,
Where mis-devotion doth command,
    Then, he that digges us up, will bring
    Us, to the Bishop, and the King,
        To make us Reliques; then
Thou shalt be'a Mary Magdalen, and I

A something else thereby;
All women shall adore us, and some men;
And since at such times, miracles are sought,
I would that age were by this paper taught
What miracles wee harmlesse lovers wrought.

First, we lov'd well and faithfully,
Yet knew not what wee lov'd, nor why,
Difference of sex no more wee knew
Than our Guardian Angells doe;
Comming and going, wee
Perchance might kisse, but not between those meales;
Our hands ne'er touch't the seales,
Which nature, injur'd by late law, sets free:
These miracles wee did; but now alas,
All measure, and all language, I should passe,
Should I tell what a miracle shee was.

## Old Man

ED WARD  THOMAS

Old Man, or Lad's-Love, – in the name there's nothing
To one that knows not Lad's-Love, or Old Man,
The hoar-green feathery herb, almost a tree,
Growing with rosemary and lavender.
Even to one that knows it well, the names
Half decorate, half perplex, the thing it is:
At least, what that is clings not to the names
In spite of time. And yet I like the names.

The herb itself I like not, but for certain
I love it, as some day the child will love it
Who plucks a feather from the door-side bush
Whenever she goes in or out of the house.
Often she waits there, snipping the tips and shrivelling
The shreds at last on to the path, perhaps
Thinking, perhaps of nothing, till she sniffs
Her fingers and runs off. The bush is still
But half as tall as she, though it is as old;
So well she clips it. Not a word she says;
And I can only wonder how much hereafter
She will remember, with that bitter scent,
Of garden rows, and ancient damson trees
Topping a hedge, a bent path to a door,
A low thick bush beside the door, and me
Forbidding her to pick.

         As for myself,
Where first I met the bitter scent is lost.
I, too, often shrivel the grey shreds,
Sniff them and think and sniff again and try
Once more to think what it is I am remembering,
Always in vain. I cannot like the scent,
Yet I would rather give up others more sweet,
With no meaning, than this bitter one.

I have mislaid the key. I sniff the spray
And think of nothing; I see and I hear nothing;
Yet seem, too, to be listening, lying in wait
For what I should, yet never can, remember:
No garden appears, no path, no hoar-green bush
Of Lad's-Love, or Old Man, no child beside,

Neither father nor mother, nor any playmate;
Only an avenue, dark, nameless, without end.


## In Mourning Wise Since Daily I Increase

THOMAS WYATT

In Mourning wise since daily I increase,
Thus should I cloak the cause of all my grief:
So pensive mind with tongue to hold his peace,
My reason sayeth there can be no relief;
Wherefore, give ear, I humbly you require,
The affects to know that thus doth make me moan.
The cause is great of all my doleful cheer
For those that were and now be dead and gone.

What thought to death desert be now their call
As by their faults it doth appear right plain?
Of force I must lament that such a fall
Should light on those so wealthily did reign,
Though some perchance will say, of cruel heart,
'A traitor's death why should we thus bemoan?'
But I, alas, set this offence apart,
Must needs bewail the death of some be gone.

As for them all I do not thus lament
But as of right my reason doth me bind.
But as the most doth all their deaths repent,
Even so do I by force of mourning mind.
Some say, 'Rochford, hadst thou been not so proud,
For thy great wit each man would thee bemoan,'

Since as it is so, many cry aloud
'It is great loss that thou art dead and gone.'

Ah! Norris, Norris, my tears begin to run
To think what hap did thee so lead or guide,
Whereby thou hast both thee and thine undone,
That is bewailed in court of every side.
In place also where thou hast never been
Both man and child doth piteously thee moan.
They say, 'Alas, thou art far overseen
By thine offences to be thus dead and gone.'

Ah! Weston, Weston, that pleasant was and young,
In active things who might with thee compare?
All words accept that thou didst speak with tongue,
So well esteemed with each where thou didst fare.
And we that now in court doth lead our life,
Most part in mind doth thee lament and moan.
But that thy faults we daily hear so rife,
All we should weep that thou are dead and gone.

Brereton, farewell, as one that least I knew.
Great was thy love with diverse, as I hear,
But common voice doth not so sore thee rue
As other twain that doth before appear.
But yet no doubt but thy friends thee lament
And other hear their piteous cry and moan.
So doth each heart for thee likewise relent
That thou giv'st cause thus to be dead and gone.

Ah, Mark, what moan should I for thee make more
Since that thy death thou hast deserved best,

Save only that mine eye is forced sore
With piteous plaint to moan thee with the rest?
A time thou hadst above thy poor degree,
The fall whereof thy friends may well bemoan.
A rotten twig upon so high a tree
Hath slipped thy hold and thou art dead and gone.

And thus, farewell, each one in hearty wise.
The axe is home, your heads be in the street.
The trickling tears doth fall so from my eyes,
I scarce may write, my paper is so wet.
But what can help when death hath played his part
Though nature's course will thus lament and moan?
Leave sobs therefore, and every Christian heart
Pray for the souls of those be dead and gone.

## A Tocata of Galuppi's

ROBERT BROWNING

I

Oh Galuppi, Baldassaro, this is very sad to find!
I can hardly misconceive you; it would prove me deaf and
    blind;
But although I take your meaning, 'tis with such a heavy
    mind!

II

Here you come with your old music, and here's all the good it
    brings.
What, they lived once thus at Venice where the merchants

were the kings,
Where Saint Mark's is, where the Doges used to wed the sea
with rings?

### III

Ay, because the sea's the street there; and 'tis arched by... what
you call
... Shylock's bridge with houses on it, where they kept the
carnival:
I was never out of England — it's as if I saw it all.

### IV

Did young people take their pleasure when the sea was warm
in May?
Balls and masks begun at midnight, burning ever to mid-day,
When they made up fresh adventures for the morrow, do you
say?

### V

Was a lady such a lady, cheeks so round and lips so red, —
On her neck the small face buoyant, like a bell-flower on its
bed,
O'er the breast's superb abundance where a man might base
his head?

### VI

Well, and it was graceful of them — they'd break talk off and
afford
— She, to bite her mask's black velvet — he, to finger on his
sword,
While you sat and played Toccatas, stately at the clavichord?

## VII

What? Those lesser thirds so plaintive, sixths diminished, sigh
on sigh,
Told them something? Those suspensions, those solutions —
'Must we die?'
Those commiserating sevenths — 'Life might last! we can but
try!'

## VIII

'Were you happy?' — 'Yes.' — 'And are you still as happy?' —
'Yes. And you?'
— 'Then, more kisses!' — 'Did *I* stop them, when a million
seemed so few?'
Hark, the dominant's persistence till it must be answered to!

## IX

So, an octave struck the answer. Oh, they praised you, I dare
say!
'Brave Galuppi! that was music! good alike at grave and gay!
'I can always leave off talking when I hear a master play!'

## X

Then they left you for their pleasure: till in due time, one by
one,
Some with lives that came to nothing, some with deeds as well
undone,
Death stepped tacitly and took them where they never see the
sun.

## XI

But when I sit down to reason, think to take my stand nor
swerve,

While I triumph o'er a secret wrung from nature's close
  reserve,
In you come with your cold music till I creep through every
  nerve.

### XII

Yes, you, like a ghostly cricket, creaking where a house was
  burned:
'Dust and ashes, dead and done with, Venice spent what
  Venice earned.
'The soul, doubtless, is immortal — where a soul can be dis-
  cerned.

### XIII

'Yours for instance: you know physics, something of geology,
'Mathematics are your pastime; souls shall rise in their degree;
'Butterflies may dread extinction, — you'll not die, it cannot
  be!

### XIV

'As for Venice and her people, merely born to bloom and
  drop,
'Here on earth they bore their fruitage, mirth and folly were
  the crop:
'What of soul was left, I wonder, when the kissing had to stop?

### XV

'Dust and ashes!' So you creak it, and I want the heart to scold.
Dear dead women, with such hair, too — what's become of all
  the gold
Used to hang and brush their bosoms? I feel chilly and grown old.

## Ode on a Grecian Urn

JOHN KEATS

Thou still unravish'd bride of quietness,
　　Thou foster-child of silence and slow time,
Sylvan historian, who canst thus express
　　A flowery tale more sweetly than our rhyme:
What leaf-fring'd legend haunts about thy shape
　　Of deities or mortals, or of both,
　　　　In Tempe or the dales of Arcady?
　　What men or gods are these? What maidens loth?
What mad pursuit? What struggle to escape?
　　　　What pipes and timbrels? What wild ecstasy?

Heard melodies are sweet, but those unheard
　　Are sweeter; therefore, ye soft pipes, play on;
Not to the sensual ear, but, more endear'd,
　　Pipe to the spirit ditties of no tone:
Fair youth, beneath the trees, thou canst not leave
　　Thy song, nor ever can those trees be bare;
　　　　Bold Lover, never, never canst thou kiss,
Though winning near the goal – yet, do not grieve;
　　She cannot fade, though thou hast not thy bliss,
　　　　For ever wilt thou love, and she be fair!

Ah, happy, happy boughs! that cannot shed
　　Your leaves, nor ever bid the Spring adieu;
And, happy melodist, unwearied,
　　For ever piping songs for ever new;
More happy love! more happy, happy love!

For ever warm and still to be enjoy'd,
　　For ever panting, and for ever young;
All breathing human passion far above,
　　That leaves a heart high-sorrowful and cloy'd,
　　　　A burning forehead, and a parching tongue.

Who are these coming to the sacrifice?
　　To what green altar, O mysterious priest,
Lead'st thou that heifer lowing at the skies,
　　And all her silken flanks with garlands drest?
What little town by river or sea shore,
　　Or mountain-built with peaceful citadel,
　　　　Is emptied of this folk, this pious morn?
And, little town, thy streets for evermore
　　Will silent be; and not a soul to tell
　　　　Why thou art desolate, can e'er return.

O Attic shape! Fair attitude! with brede
　　Of marble men and maidens overwrought,
With forest branches and the trodden weed;
　　Thou, silent form, dost tease us out of thought
As doth eternity: Cold Pastoral!
　　When old age shall this generation waste,
　　Thou shalt remain, in midst of other woe
Than ours, a friend to man, to whom thou say'st,
　　'Beauty is truth, truth beauty,—that is all
　　　　Ye know on earth, and all ye need to know.'

## *Polonius*

MIROSLAV HOLUB

Behind every arras
he does his duty
unswervingly.
Walls are his ears,
keyholes his eyes.

He slinks up the stairs,
oozes from the ceiling,
floats through the door
ready to give evidence,
prove what is proven,
stab with a needle
or pin on an order.

His poems always rhyme,
his brush is dipped in honey,
his music flutes
from marzipan and cane.

You buy him
by weight, boneless,
a pound of wax flesh,
a pound of mousy philosophy,
a pound of jellied
flunkey.

And when he's sold out

and the left-overs wrapped
in a tasselled obituary,
a paranoid funeral notice,

and when the spore-creating mould
of memory
covers him over,
when he falls
arse-first to the stars,

the whole continent will be lighter,
earth's axis straighten up
and in night's thunderous arena
a bird will chirp in gratitude.


## Very Simply Topping Up the Brake Fluid

SIMON ARMITAGE

Yes, love, that's why the warning light comes on. Don't
panic. Fetch some universal brake-fluid
and a five-eighths screwdriver from your toolkit
then prop the bonnet open. Go on, it won't

eat you. Now, without slicing through the fan-belt
try and slide the sharp end of the screwdriver
under the lid and push the spade connector
through its bed, go on, that's it. Now you're all right

to unscrew, no, clockwise, you see it's Russian
love, back to front, that's it. You see, it's empty.

Now, gently with your hand and I mean gently,
try and create a bit of space by pushing

the float-chamber sideways so there's room to pour,
gently does it, that's it. Try not to spill it, it's
corrosive: rusts, you know, and fill it till it's
level with the notch on the clutch reservoir.

Lovely. There's some Swarfega in the office
if you want a wash and some soft roll above
the cistern for, you know. Oh don't mind him, love,
he doesn't bite. Come here and sit down Prince. Prince!

Now, where's that bloody alternator? Managed?
Oh any time, love. I'll not charge you for that
because it's nothing of a job. If you want
us again we're in the book. Tell your husband.


## *Never Mind the Quality:*

SIMON ARMITAGE

feel the width.
But how many times
had she worked the blade
of a paper-scraper
under a loose length
of faded paper and pulled,
only to see it shear,
or tear, or taper out

like the roots of a tree
or the source of a river?
More times than she cared
to remember. Of all days
it was Sunday.
One small corner
of the parlour wall
had peeled away

and she folded it back
like the finishing touch
to a well-made bed,
then took it in hand
and simply she used
her own weight, leant right out
like a wind-surfer rounding
the tip of Cape Horn

and it came
and kept coming, breathtaking,
like a seam of ore
through an unclaimed mountain –
from the skirting board
to the picture rail,
from the door frame
to the bay window.

Her man was adamant;
he would not have it
in the house,
would not dream of it.
Not on the creel

with his damp linen, no way.
Not near the hob
where his bread was rising,
not in the porch
where the grouse were hanging,
not on the couch, spread
like an antimacassar
of some measure.
In short, not nowhere.
Out it went, over the line
like a starched sheet

or an old tent
strung out for airing.
The word went round.
She of all people
had stripped a piece
the size of a bedspread.
A double bed
someone enlarged; a gable end

added another.
They gathered in the market
to trade stories,
held out their arms
as if it were
a fish, a pike, the one
that got away,
or so much cloth,

or a monster putt
from off the green – the ball

that teased the rim
of the cup then stopped
and dropped, sweet
as a nut, sunk.
The men could lip-read.
From their sinks and stoves
they looked up, undid
their aprons, kicked off
their slippers
and jumped in their brogues,
then slopped outside
with a bucket and brush
to swill down their flags
and watch their women.

It was dropping dark
and words were difficult
to see. 'This big, sisters,'
said one girl, her arms
and fingers spread, as if
relieved of a great cat's cradle
or ready for several feet
of fine imaginary yarn.

## Cows

PAUL MULDOON

———

Even as we speak, there's a smoker's cough
from behind the whitethorn hedge: we stop dead in our
     tracks;

a distant tingle of water into a trough.

———

In the past half-hour—since a cattle truck
all but sent us shuffling off this mortal coil—
we've consoled ourselves with the dregs

of a bottle of Redbreast. Had Hawthorne been a Gael,
I insist, the scarlet 'A' on Hester Prynne
would have stood for 'Alcohol'.

This must be the same truck whose tail-lights burn
so dimly, as if caked with dirt,
three or four hundred yards along the boreen

(a diminutive form of the Gaelic *bóthar*, 'a road',
from *bó*, 'a cow,' and *thar*
meaning, in this case, something like 'athwart',

'boreen' has entered English 'through the air'
despite the protestations of the O.E.D.):
why, though, should one tail-light flash and flare,

then flicker-fade
to an afterimage of tourmaline
set in a dark part-jet, part-jasper or -jade?

———

That smoker's cough again: it triggers off from drumlin
to drumlin an emphysemantiphon
of cows. They hoist themselves on to their trampoline

and steady themselves and straight away divine
water in some far-flung spot
to which they then gravely incline. This is no Devon

cow-coterie, by the way, whey-faced, with Spode
hooves and horns: nor are they the metaphysicattle of Japan
that have merely to anticipate

scoring a bull's-eye and, lo, it happens;
these are earth-flesh, earth-blood, salt of the earth,
whose talismans are their own jaw-bones

buried under threshold and hearth.
For though they trace themselves to the kith and kine
that presided over the birth

of Christ (so carry their calves a full nine
months and boast liquorice
cachous on their tongues), they belong more to the line

that's tramped these cwms and corries
since Cuchulainn tramped Aoife.
Again the flash. Again the fade. However I might allegorize

some oscaraboscarabinary bevy
of cattle there's no getting round this cattle-truck,
one light on the blink, laden with what? Microwaves? Hi-fis?

———

*Oscaraboscarabinary*: a twin, entwined, a tree, a Tuareg;
a double dung-beetle; a plain
and simple hi-firing party; an off-the-back-of-a-lorry drogue?

Enough of Colette and Céline, Céline and Paul Celan:
enough of whether Nabokov
taught at Wellesley or Wesleyan.

Now let us talk of slaughter and the slain,
the helicopter gun-ship, the mighty Kalashnikov:
let's rest for a while in a place where a cow has lain.

# Acknowledgements

The author and publisher would like to thank the following for permission to reproduce copyright material:

Acocella, Joan, 'Prophet Motive', *New Yorker* (7 January 2008)

Adcock, Fleur, 'Not Quite a Statement' in *Strong Words* (Bloodaxe Books, 2000), reprinted by permission of Bloodaxe Books

Amis, Martin, *The Pregnant Widow* (Jonathan Cape, 2010), reprinted by permission of The Wylie Agency

Ansen, Alan, *The Table Talk of W. H. Auden* (Faber & Faber, 1990), reprinted by permission of Faber & Faber Ltd

Armitage, Simon, 'Very Simply Topping Up the Brake Fluid' in *Zoom!* (Bloodaxe Books, 2014), and 'Never Mind the Quality' in *Kid* (Faber & Faber, 2002), reprinted by permission of the author

Aslam, Nadeem, 'Leila in the Wilderness' in *Granta* 112 (Granta, 2010)

Auden, W.H., 'Autumn Song' and 'Night Mail', in *Poems of Freedom*, ed. John Mulgan (Random House, 1947), reprinted by permission of Random House and Curtis Brown

Baker, Nicholson, *The Anthologist* (Simon & Schuster, 2009), reprinted by permission of the author

Banville, John, from 'The Still Mysterious Enchanter', *The New York Review of Books* (NYRP, 15 July 2010), reprinted by permission of *The New York Review of Books*

Barnes, Julian, *Nothing to Be Frightened Of* (Random House, 2008), reprinted by permission of Vintage Books

Bate, Jonathan, *Cambridge Companion to Creative Writing* (Cambridge University Press, 2012)

Bauby, Jean-Dominique, *The Diving-Bell and the Butterfly* (HarperCollins,

1988), reprinted by permission of HarperCollins Publishers Ltd

Bellow, Saul, *The Adventures of Augie March* (Penguin, 2012); *Henderson the Rain King* (Penguin, 1999); *Humboldt's Gift* (Penguin, 2007), reprinted by permission of Penguin Random House

Bigsby, Christopher, programme note for *Who's Afraid of Virginia Woolf?* (Almeida Theatre, 1996)

Bishop, Elizabeth, 'The Bight' (Macmillan, 1948); *Christian Science Monitor* (Macmillan, 1979); *Prose: The Centenary Edition* (Random House, 2014); *Key West Notebook II* (Vassar College Library and Farrar, Straus & Giroux, 1934)

Borges, Jorge Luis, 'The Art of Fiction No. 39', in *The Paris Review* No. 40 (Spring-Summer, 1957) reprinted by permission of *The Paris Review*

Bragg, Melvyn, *A Time to Dance* (Hodder, 2012)

Brodsky, Joseph, 'Centaurs I', and 'Clouds', 'So Forth', in *So Forth* (Macmillan, 1996); *Watermark* (Macmillan, 2013); 'The Sound of the Tide', in *Less Than One: Selected Essays* (Penguin, 2011); Nobel Prize acceptance speech (World Scientific/Nobel Prize, 1987)

Carey, John, *What Good are the Arts?* (Faber & Faber, 2006)

Carson, Ciaran, 'Cocktails' in *The Irish for No* (The Gallery Press, 1987), reprinted by permission of the author and The Gallery Press

Carson, Anne, Interview on *Start the Week* (Radio 4, 30 September 2013); 'Irony is not Enough: Essay on my Life as Catherine Deneuve' (Fragment31, 2010)

Chekhov, Anton, *The Kiss* (Duckworth & Co., 1908), *My Life* and *The Teacher of Literature* (Adolf Marx, 1901)

Cope, Wendy, at Salisbury Literary Festival (Faber & Faber, 2001), reprinted by permission of the author

Creeley, Robert, 'Hotel Lobby', in *The Collected Poems of Robert Creeley, 1975–2005*, vol. 2 (University of California Press, 2008)

Davies, R. T., *Medieval English Lyrics* (Faber & Faber, 1963), reprinted by permission of Faber & Faber

Dickinson, Emily, 'I could bring You Jewels' (1863), 'He fumbles at your Soul', 'I never lost as much but twice' and 'I'll tell you how the Sun rose' (1862), in *The Poems of Emily Dickinson*, edited by Thomas H. Johnson, Cambridge, Mass. (The Belknap Press of Harvard University Press), reprinted by permission of the publishers and the Trustees of Amherst College. Copyright © 1951, 1955 by the President and Fellows of Harvard College. Copyright © renewed 1979, 1983 by the President and Fellows of Harvard College. Copyright © 1914, 1918, 1919, 1924, 1929,1930, 1932, 1935, 1937, 1942, by Martha Dickinson Bianchi. Copyright © 1952, 1957, 1958, 1963, 1965, by Mary L. Hampson.

Duffy, Carol Ann, 'Stuffed', in *Collected Poems* (Picador, 2015), reprinted by permission of the author

Eliot, T. S., Review in the *TLS* of *Metaphysical Lyrics and Poems of the Seventeenth Century: Donne to Butler*, ed. Herbert Grierson (Times Literary Supplement, October 1921); Preface to *Collected Poems* by Harold Monro (Faber & Faber, 1933); 'Tradition and the Individual Talent' (Faber & Faber, 1919), 'The Music of Poetry' (Faber & Faber, 1942); *On Poetry and Poets* (Faber & Faber, 1957); 'The Metaphysical Poets' (*Times Literary Supplement*, October 1921); 'Burnt Norton', *Four Quartets* (Faber & Faber, 1936); 'The Lovesong of J. Alfred Prufrock', *Selected Poems of T. S. Eliot (Faber 80th Anniversary Edition)* (Faber & Faber, 2009); *Murder in the Cathedral* (Faber & Faber, 1973); 'Portrait of A Lady', 'Poetry and Drama', *Selected Poems of T. S. Eliot (Faber 80th Anniversary Edition)* (Faber & Faber, 2009); *The Use of Poetry and the Use of Criticism* (Faber & Faber, 1986); *Speculations* in *The Use of Poetry* (Faber & Faber, 1938); *On Poetry and Poets* (Faber & Faber, 1957); 'Dante', *Selected Prose of T. S. Eliot* (Faber & Faber, 1929); 'The Perfect Critic', *The Sacred Wood: Essays on Poetry and Criticism* (Faber & Faber, 1997), reprinted by permission of the Eliot Estate and Faber & Faber

Fantoni, Barry, 'Lines on the Return to Britain of Billy Graham',

(*Private Eye*, 1987), reprinted by permission of *Private Eye*

Farmelo, Graham, *The Strangest Man* (Faber & Faber, 2009), reprinted by permission of Faber & Faber

Fenton, James, 'Lines for Translation into Any Language' and 'A German Requiem', *Children in Exile: Poems 1968–1984* (FSG, 1994), reprinted by permission of the author

Flaubert, Gustave, 'Letter to Louise Colet' (15 July 1853)

Forster, E. M., *The Longest Journey* (Blackwood, 1907), reprinted by permission of The Society of Authors

Foulds, Adam, extract from *The Guardian* (25 January 2014)

Frost, Robert, 'Stopping by Woods on a Snowy Evening', 'A Patch of Old Snow', 'Now Close the Windows', 'Good Hours', and 'New Hampshire', in *The Collected Poems* (Vintage, 2013)

Gardner, Helen, *The Art of T. S. Eliot* (Faber & Faber, 1968), reprinted by permission of Faber & Faber

Gogol, Nikolai, *Dead Souls* (Oxford University Press, 1971)

Golding, William, *Darkness Visible* (Faber & Faber, 1981); *Lord of the Flies* (Faber & Faber, 1963); *Pincher Martin* (Faber & Faber, 1973), reprinted by permission of Faber & Faber and the Golding Estate

Haffenden, John, *Viewpoints: Poets in Conversation with John Haffenden* (Faber & Faber, 1981), reprinted by permission of Faber & Faber

Hamilton, Ian, 'In Conversation with Peter Dale', in *Agenda 31.2* (Agenda 31.2, 1993); *Fifty Poems* (Faber & Faber, 1988), reprinted by permission of Faber & Faber

Haughton, Hugh, *The Poetry of Derek Mahon* (OUP, 2010), reprinted by permission of Oxford University Press

Heaney, Seamus, 'Kinship', 'Funeral Rites', and 'The Gravel Walks' in *Spirit Level* (Faber & Faber, 1996); 'A Dream of Jealousy' in *Field The Government of the Tongue* (Faber & Faber, 1996), reprinted by permission of Faber & Faber and the Heaney Estate

Herbert, Zbigniew, 'Arion', and 'Three Studies on the Subject of Realism', in *The Collected Poems 1956–1998* (Atlantic Books, 2014), reprinted by permission of Atlantic Books

Hickling, Alfred, 'Border Crossings', *The Guardian* (2 October 2007), reprinted by permission of *The Guardian*

Hill, Geoffrey, 'September Song', 'The Humanist', and 'Funeral Music' in *Broken Hierachies* (OUP, 2013)

Holub, Miroslav, 'Polonius', *Selected Poems*, (Bloodaxe Books, 1967); *The Dimension of the Present Moment*, (Faber & Faber, 1990), reprinted by permission of Faber & Faber

Housman, A. E., 'Tell Me Not Here', *Last Poems*, (Project Gutenburg, 1922); 'letter to Seymour Adelman' (6 May 1926), reprinted by permission of The Society of Authors as the Literary Representative of the Estate of A. E. Housman

Hughes, Ted, 'New Year exhilaration', *Collected Poems of Ted Hughes*, (Faber & Faber, 2003); 'Snow smoking as the fields boil' in *Moortown Diary* (Faber & Faber, 1979); *Poetry in the Making* (Faber & Faber, 2008), reprinted by permission of Faber & Faber and the Hughes Estate

Jones, Brian, *Poems* (London Magazine Editions, 1967), reprinted by permission of *The London Magazine*

Kendall, Tim, *Paul Muldoon* (Seren, 1996), reprinted by permission of Seren Books

Kipling, Rudyard, 'Harp Song of the Dane Women', in *The Cambridge Edition of the Poems of Rudyard Kipling* (Cambridge University Press, 2013)

Kundera, Milan, *The Unbearable Lightness of Being* (Faber & Faber, 2000); *Life is Elsewhere* (Faber & Faber, 2000); *The Art of the Novel* (Faber & Faber, 2005), reprinted by permission of Faber & Faber

Larkin, Philip, 'The Whitsun Weddings', and 'Afternoons', in *Philip Larkin: Collected Poems* (Faber & Faber, 2003), reprinted by permission of Faber & Faber

Levi, Primo, 'On Obscure Writing' (La Stampa, 1976)

Mahon, Derek, 'A Disused Shed in Co. Wexford', in *Collected Poems*

(The Gallery Press, 1975), reprinted by permission of The Gallery Press

Marquez, Gabriel Garcia, *Love in the Time of Cholera* (Random House, 1989)

Maxwell, Julie, *These Are Our Children* (Quercus, 2013), reprinted by permission of the author

Maxwell, Glyn, *On Poetry* (Oberon Books, 2013), reprinted by permission of the author

Mayakovsky, Vladimir, 'A Cloud in Trousers' (Osip Brik, 1915)

McEwan, Ian, *The Comfort of Strangers* (Random House, 2010), reprinted by permission of the author

Melville, Pauline, *Wasafiri Magazine* issue 75 (2005), reprinted by permission of the author and *Wasafiri Magazine*

Muldoon, Paul, 'Cows', 'Diogenes', 'Quoof', '7, Middagh Street', 'Vico', in *Poems 1968–1998* (Faber & Faber, 2001), reprinted by permission of the author

Nabokov, Vladimir, *Bend Sinister* (Henry Holt and Co., 1947) 'First Love', in *Nabokov's Dozen* (1958, Doubleday); *Lolita* (Olympia Press, 1955); *Speak, Memory* (Victor Gollancz, 1951)

O'Brien, Sean, *Guardian Review* (8 March 2008)

Oswald, Alice, 'A Greyhound in the Evening after a Long Day of Rain', in *The Thing in the Gap-Stone Stile* (Faber & Faber, 2006), reprinted by permission of Faber & Faber

Paulin, Tom, *The Secret Life of Poems* (Faber & Faber, 2011); *Minotaur* (Faber & Faber, 1992), reprinted by permission of Faber & Faber

Plath, Sylvia, *The Bell Jar* (Faber & Faber, 1966); 'Ariel', 'Last Words', 'Mystic', 'By Candlelight', and 'Wuthering Heights', in *Collected Poems* (Faber & Faber, 2002); Radio 3, speaking about 'Sheep in Fog' (1963), reprinted by permission of Faber & Faber and the Plath Estate

Pound, Ezra, 'In a Station of the Metro', and 'Papyrus', in *Selected Poems and Translations* (Faber & Faber, 2011), reprinted by permission of Faber & Faber

Raine, Craig, 'A Martian Sends a Postcard Home' (Oxford University Press, 1979), reprinted by permission of the author

Reid, Christopher, 'Ivesian Fugue', and 'A Whole School of Bourgeois Primitives', in *Pea Soup* (OUP, 1982), reprinted by permission of the author

Ricks, Christopher, 'The Mouth, the Meal and the Book' (*London Review of Books*, 8 November 1979), reprinted by permission of the author and *London Review of Books*

Solt, Andrew, *Imagine: John Lennon* (produced and directed for Warner Bros., 1988), reprinted by permission of Andrew Solt

Stevens, Wallace, 'Adagia', *Opus Posthumous* (Faber & Faber, 1990), reprinted by permission of Faber & Faber

Stevenson, Anne, *Poetry* (Bloodaxe Books, 2007), reprinted by permission of Bloodaxe Books

Stoppard, Tom, 'Playwrights and Professors', first published in *The Times Literary Supplement* on 1 October 1972 and reprinted by permission of the *TLS*

Stravinsky, Igor, *Autobiography* (Alma Books, 2013), and reprinted by permission of Alma Books

Thomas, Dylan, 'Fern Hill', 'A Refusal to Mourn the Death, by Fire, of a Child in London', and 'Fern Hill', in *The Collected Poems of Dylan Thomas: The New Centenary Edition* (Weidenfeld & Nicolson, 2014), reprinted by permission of the David Higham Group

Thomas, Edward, 'Old Man', in *Selected Poems of Edward Thomas* (Faber & Faber, 2011), reprinted by permission of Faber & Faber

University of California Museum of Palaeontology, 'Introduction to Ctenophora' (University of California, 2015), reprinted by permission of the University of California Museum of Palaeontology

Updike, John, *Rabbit Redux* (Penguin Classics, 2006); *Of the Farm* (Penguin Classics, 2007); *More Matter: Essays and Criticism* (Penguin, 2000), reprinted by permission of Penguin Books Ltd

Valéry, Paul, 'Analects', in *Collected Works of Paul Valery*, vol. 14, ed. Jackson Mathews and Kegan Paul, extracted from *Tel Quel* © Editions Gallimard, Paris, 1935 et 1943; and 'Concerning Le cimetière marin', extracted from 'Charmes' in *Poésie* © Editions Gallimard, Paris, 1922 et 1929 (Routledge, 1970), reprinted with the permission of Editions Gallimard

Wagner, Erica, 'Don't Think, Just Feel', *The Times* (12 November 2005), reprinted by permission of the author

Walcott, Derek, interviewed by Tom Payne in *The Telegraph* (22 January 2011); 'Another Life', in *The Poetry of Derek Walcott 1948–2013* (Faber & Faber, 1973); 'Store Boy', in *The Fortunate Traveller* (Faber & Faber, 1982); 'Another Life', 'The Schooner Flight', and 'Omeros', in *The Poetry of Derek Walcott 1948–2013* (Faber & Faber, 2014), reprinted by permission of Faber & Faber

Whitman, Walt, 'Sparkles from the Wheel', 'The Torch', and 'Song of Myself', in *Leaves of Grass*, (1855)

Williams, William Carlos, 'The Red Wheelbarrow', and 'The Last Words of My English Grandmother', in *The Collected Poems: Volume I, 1909–1939* (ND Books, 1938); 'A Sort of a Song', in *The Collected Poems: Volume II, 1939–1962*, (ND Books, 1944); 'On Measure – Statement for Cid Corman', in *Selected Essays of William Carlos Williams* (ND Books, 1954), reprinted by permission of New Directions Publishing Corp.

Williams, C. K., 'Reading the Cop', in *Flesh and Blood* (FSG, April 1988), reprinted by permission of the author

Wills, Clair, *Reading Paul Muldoon* (Bloodaxe Books, 1997), reprinted by permission of Bloodaxe Books

Wilson, Edmund, *Axel's Castle* (FSG, 1961)

Wood, James, *How Fiction Works* (Random House, 2009)

Wroe, Nicholas, 'Food for the soul, from Eliot to the hermit of Hull', *The Guardian* (11 March 2008), reprinted by permission of the author

Tamsin Shelton copy-edited this book. The author would like to express his amazement and gratitude for her swiftness, her unsleeping efficiency, her tenacity and unfailing intelligence.